POPULAR MUSIC WILL NOT SAVE US

COUNTERPOINTS: MUSIC AND EDUCATION

Randall Everett Allsup, editor

POPULAR MUSIC WILL NOT SAVE US

Capitalism and Music Education

LAUREN KAPALKA RICHERME

INDIANA UNIVERSITY PRESS

This book is a publication of

Indiana University Press
Office of Scholarly Publishing
Herman B Wells Library 350
1320 East 10th Street
Bloomington, Indiana 47405 USA

iupress.org

First Printing 2025

Cataloging information is available from the Library of Congress.

ISBN 978-0-253-07243-6 (cloth)
ISBN 978-0-253-07244-3 (paperback)
ISBN 978-0-253-07246-7 (epub)
ISBN 978-0-253-07245-0 (ebook PDF)

CONTENTS

PREFACE

TO BE PART OF A society is to be part of an economy. While various forms of economic exchange have evolved throughout the world over the past few millennia, most humans now reside within capitalist systems. How and to what extent capitalism influences aspects of individuals' lives, including educational practices and cultural opportunities, varies from place to place and changes over time. Whether consciously or unconsciously, humans continually position themselves in relation to capitalist practices through a combination of thriving within, surviving under, and perhaps resisting or directly challenging them.

At first glance, it may seem obvious that music education practices occur in integration with economic ones. Institutions ranging from royal courts to places of worship have long supported professional musicians, and contemporary music educators may find themselves compensated by schools, private students, government grants, or community-based organizations, to name a few. While questions about who does and should financially support contemporary music education efforts deserve attention, economic practices influence more than just finances.

Values underlying everyday life, such as competition and cooperation, function inseparably from economic systems. When a student in a capitalist society competes in a solo music performance event, the experience reinforces the individual's identity as a musician and as a member of—and perhaps current or future worker in—that society. These interconnected aspects of students' and teachers' selves can foster long-standing, relatively immobile values and dispositions. bell hooks argues that "the imprints of a consumer capitalist socialization that teaches us all to spend much and value little, to get as much as we can and give as little as possible . . . cannot be erased at will."[1]

Alterations within economic systems may impact not only financial engagements and individual identities but also interpersonal relationships and ethical ideals. As David Harvey explains, studying how capitalism influences daily life illuminates aspects of individuals' relationships with nature, technology, and one another as well as cognitive schemes that inform and ultimately limit ways of knowing the world.[2] In short, capitalism does not just underlie twenty-first-century societies and individuals—it constitutes them.

Additionally, relatively recent technological changes, such as the widespread adoption of smartphones and social media platforms, promote permeable boundaries between leisure activities—which often involve capitalist consumption—and capitalist work endeavors.[3] What were once largely local activities, such as participating in a community ukulele group, may now function as opportunities for self-branding and self-promotion on social media that can enhance a music maker's broader social standing and employability.

The idea that economic forces and values necessarily influence institutions, individuals, and social relations, including music education practices, may seem too obvious and inevitable to consider further. Throughout the process of writing this book, I felt like a fish trying to describe water. I have spent so long metaphorically swimming in capitalist systems that I struggled to understand how such practices inform both my ways of being in the world and my imagining of possible alternative actions.

More broadly, this book project continues my exploration of a provocation posed to me by an undergraduate mentor: What should the relationship between society and music education be? While I have grappled with this question in various publications, including my book *Complicating, Considering, and Connecting Music Education,* that work provides little attention to how economic practices interface with music educators' current and potential future values and actions. Music educators can complicate, consider, and connect without ever attending to the economic systems that correspond with and bound their practices.

While capitalist economic systems have informed humans' actions and values for centuries, a couple of concerning contemporary trends make attention to these systems crucially important. Income inequality in the United States and elsewhere has grown over the past half century. CEO earnings have increased to more than three hundred times the wages of average workers, and when adjusted for inflation, most workers' earnings have changed little in the past four decades.[4] Additionally, regional convergence in per capita incomes in the United States has ceased; while in previous decades, the standard of living in states with lower incomes (such as Mississippi) rose in comparison to that in states with higher incomes (like Massachusetts), vast economic disparities between states have now stabilized.[5]

As the United States continues exporting economic policies throughout the world, social inequality has grown to staggering levels.[6] In addition to owning private jets and three hundred-foot yachts, the global elite has been known to pay $24 million USD to hire Beyoncé for private concerts.[7] In contrast, 719 million people—about 9.2 percent of the global population—currently live on less than $2.15 USD per day.[8]

Many view education as the sole solution to socioeconomic disparities. However, since contemporary globalized capitalism relies on paying workers as little as possible, changed curriculum content, higher standards, and added job training alone will not minimize growing material inequities. Educational attainment can alter individuals' economic standing, but because it leaves the capitalist premise that societies demand financial winners and losers unquestioned, it merely shuffles who thrives and faulters, still predestining the vast global majority to lifelong poverty. As Nobel Prize winning economist Paul Krugman observes, focusing on education "suggests that nobody is to blame for rising inequality."[9]

Economic trends have implications not only for teachers' and students' material circumstances but also for political processes more broadly. Krugman summarizes: "Political polarization has marched side by side with economic polarization, as income inequality has soared."[10] Political polarization makes governments less and less able to address growing economic inequities. Those feeling increasingly left behind in societies that valorize individual economic success above all else have reason to feel apathy for democratic institutions not currently serving their needs. Noting his agreement with Alan Greenspan, who Republican Ronald Reagan appointed chair of the United States Federal Reserve, Krugman asserts: "Growing inequality poses a threat to 'democratic society.'"[11]

For decades, critiques of capitalism have played a role in education philosophies, perhaps most notably those of Michael Apple.[12] Two recent musicology books, Timothy Taylor's *Music and Capitalism: A History of the Present* and Marianna Ritchey's *Composing Capital: Classical Music in the Neoliberal Era*, center on the relationship between various current music practices and capitalism. Music education scholars illuminate relationships between economic practices and standardized teaching practices and aims,[13] competitive rankings,[14] and the advancement of commercial interests.[15] Joseph Abramo and Vincent Bates trouble the lack of attention to class within music education, with the latter emphasizing the neglect of music making often favored by poor, rural, white individuals.[16]

While the impact of capitalism on music education, including as it relates to socioeconomic class, plays an important role in contemporary critical theory scholarship, philosophers tend to focus on oppression related to disability, gender, and race. Yet capitalist economic practices and their associated values reinforce ableism, racism, sexism, and other problematic divides. In hooks's words: "Class matters. Race and gender can be used as screens to deflect attention away from the harsh realities class politics exposes. Clearly, just when we should all be paying attention to class, using race and gender to understand and explain its new dimensions, society, even our government, says let's talk about race and racial injustice."[17] The knowledge and dispositions needed to combat racism and other forms of oppression may have minimal material impact in the face of widespread economic inequities and exploitation sustained by contemporary globalized capitalist practices.

Having explained the capitalism part of my title, I now address the phrase "popular music will not save us." One might wonder why I am picking on popular music. Readers may assume that in suggesting a critique of popular music, I am defending the Western music canon and Eurocentric music practices. This is not my intent. As a longtime member of progressive music education circles like the MayDay Group, I largely support the inclusion of popular music and other culturally relevant genres in music classrooms. I begin almost all of my undergraduate and graduate classes at Indiana University by examining the different musical practices in which students engage and emphasizing that I welcome and encourage attention to various forms of music making. Yet attending to capitalist systems provides opportunities to critically examine why and how teachers enact popular music–related practices.

At stake in the phrase "popular music will not save us" is not so much "popular music" as "save." I worry that, though usually well intentioned, music educators have come to understand popular music as an ethically good alternative to Western art music practices. In addition to sharing many of the same limitations in relation to capitalism as Western art music practices, popular music practices potentially reinforce key capitalist values, such as ongoing consumption, that Western art music making typically resists. Ultimately, I argue that no form of music making in and of itself can save music educators and students from the problematic aspects of contemporary capitalism. Rather, music educators and students might consider how they position themselves and their context-specific music-making practices in relation to capitalist aims and processes, including through confrontation of unethical aspects of capitalism.

I begin chapter 1 of this book with an explanation of what distinguishes capitalism from other economic systems. I offer a brief history of capitalism, including its links to eighteenth-century Europe, and then explain the role of neoliberalism in contemporary capitalism. Since the 1970s, neoliberal politicians in the United States from both liberal and conservative political parties have embraced practices that privatize public ownership, reduce the social state, and deregulate capital. After summarizing how music educators have addressed neoliberalism within the profession, I turn to the largely undiscussed topic of the capitalist subject. Following Michel Foucault, I understand capitalism as not only a system in which individuals participate but also a set of relations that produces individuals.[18] Finally, I turn to problems of contemporary globalized capitalism, including the undermining of collective responsibility and the equating of personal choice with ethical decision-making.

In chapter 2, I illuminate how progressive music education practices that center relevance and flexibility correspond to key aspects of capitalism. Relevant music-making practices often rely on youth culture, cultural omnivorousness, and attention holding, all of which further the capitalist aim of spurring consumption. Additionally, arguments related to fostering flexible musical expertise parallel the capitalist need for versatile, precarious workers. I detail limits of centering musical relevance and flexible musicianship, including promoting individualism over cooperative solidarity, emphasizing issues of recognition rather than distribution, and equating capitalist market practices with ethical action. After exploring whether certain musical practices have more potential to challenge problematic aspects of capitalism than others, I conclude by proposing the need to start from ethical, rather than musical, considerations.

Given that no musical genre inherently challenges problematic aspects of capitalism, in chapter 3 I argue that music educators might instead focus on affect. After explaining affect theory and distinguishing it from pervasive understandings about emotion in music education, I articulate how affective flows—a term used to emphasize the circulating nature of affect—can mirror the continual expansion of capitalist growth. Yet affective flows can also promote personal fulfillment and interpersonal sensational experiences as well as disruptive experiences with the potential to raise awareness about capitalist inequities. Since music educators and students might foreground ethical considerations rather than certain musical genres or practices, the second half of the chapter examines which ethical commitments could best counter problematic aspects of contemporary globalized capitalism.[19] These include valuing greater material equity and resonant engagements.

In chapters 4 through 7, I consider the possibilities of enacting music teaching and learning to promote one of four positions: thriving within, surviving under, resisting, and challenging capitalism, respectively. These chapters follow a parallel format. Each begins by using various authors' work to define the position and distinguish it from commonplace music teaching and learning practices. Subsequently, I explain the affective flows that promote the selected position. Accelerating and expanding affective flows can contribute to more robust thriving within capitalist systems, while playful affective flows might encourage more meaningful survival. Dialogic affective flows can promote the cooperative resisting of capitalist inequities, and disruptive affective flows might facilitate the challenging of capitalist inequities. Since writing can also induce artistic affective flows, sections of each chapter include poetic language meant to foster such sensations.

Focusing on more ethical action, in each of these four chapters I also consider the following question: What would centering greater material equity and resonant engagements within each positionality mean for music education endeavors? While the confines of book formatting necessitate that these four chapters appear sequentially—moving from thriving to surviving to resisting to challenging—readers can approach them in any order. At the end of each chapter, I encourage readers to pick which positionality they would like to explore next.

The final chapter of the text returns to considerations about genre. While music educators and students should refrain from understanding certain musical practices as ethical in and of themselves, avoiding considerations about styles and genres can lead to problematic exclusions and unquestioned retainment of familiar habits. I investigate how musical genres students find relevant, including popular music making, might contribute toward thriving within, surviving under, resisting, and challenging capitalism.

My exploration into capitalism has been a difficult and often troubling process. While doing research for this book, I purchased a copy of Karl Marx's *Das Kapital* on Amazon. In seeking to read Marx, I supported Amazon leaders' unacceptable treatment of employees[20] and added a few cents to Amazon founder Jeff Bezos's $206.7 billion USD net worth (which will almost certainly have grown by the time you read this sentence) without second thought. Reflecting on this exchange, I realized that capitalism has in many ways already won. Despite my efforts to think critically about the limits of capitalism, I am enmeshed in and reliant on capitalist practices that further inequities. I find resonance with Ritchey's statement: "We are all simply trying to survive, and we are all complicit in allowing capitalism to continue as we are individually helpless to stop it."[21]

While I wish that I could provide readers a completely hopeful conclusion and clear call for revolution, my explorations do not lend easily to such closure. This work, however, differs from my previous book in that it makes a normative claim. In defining greater material equity and resonant engagements as two values that can counter key pernicious aspects of contemporary globalized capitalism, I make clear assertions about actions music educators and students should take. I also empower readers to situate themselves within and among four potential positionalities: thriving within, surviving under, resisting, and challenging capitalism. Instead of relying on popular music or any other set of musical practices to save us, music educators and students might continually select ethically informed positionalities in relation to capitalist practices.

NOTES

1. bell hooks, *Where We Stand: Class Matters* (New York: Routledge, 2000), 157.
2. David Harvey, *A Companion to Marx's Capital: The Complete Edition* (Brooklyn: Verso Books, 2018), 195.
3. Aubrey Anable, "Labor/Leisure," in *Time: A Vocabulary of the Present*, ed. Joel Burges and Amy J. Elias (New York: New York University Press, 2016), 193.
4. Paul Krugman, *Arguing with Zombies* (New York: W. W. Norton, 2021), 259.
5. Krugman, *Arguing with Zombies*, 292.
6. Harvey, *Companion to Marx's Capital*, 173; Naomi Klein, *The Shock Doctrine* (New York: Metropolitan Books, 2007).
7. Evan Osnos, "How to Hire a Pop Star for Your Private Party," *New Yorker*, May 29, 2023, https://www.newyorker.com/magazine/2023/06/05/how-to-hire-a-pop-star-for-your-private-party.
8. World Vision, "Global Poverty: Facts, FAQs, and How to Help," *World Vision*, accessed June 22, 2023, https://www.worldvision.org/sponsorship-news-stories/global-poverty-facts.
9. Krugman, *Arguing with Zombies*, 292.
10. Krugman, *Arguing with Zombies*, 291.
11. Krugman, *Arguing with Zombies*, 283.
12. See, for example, Michael Apple, *Official Knowledge: Democratic Education in a Conservative Age* (New York: Routledge, 2014).
13. Randall Allsup, "The Eclipse of Higher Education or Problems Preparing Artists in a Mercantile World," *Music Education Research* 17, no. 3 (2015): 251–61; Rolando Angel-Alvarado, Bayron Gárate-González, and Isabel Quiroga-Fuentes, "Insurrection in Chile: The Effects of Neoliberalism from a Music Education Perspective," *Action, Criticism, and Theory for Music Education* 20, no. 3 (2021): 108–31; Graham McPhail and Jeff McNeill, "Music Education and the Neoliberal Turn in Aotearoa New Zealand," *Action, Criticism, and Theory for Music Education* 20, no. 3 (2021): 44–81; Jess Mullen, "Music Education for Some: Music Standards at the Nexus of Neoliberal Reforms and Neoconservative Values," *Action Criticism, and Theory for Music Education* 18, no. 1 (2019): 44–67.

14. Joseph Abramo, "The Phantasmagoria of Competition in School Ensembles," *Philosophy of Music Education Review* 23, no. 2 (2017): 150–70; Allsup, "Eclipse of Higher Education"; Sean Robert Powell, "Competition, Ideology, and the One-Dimensional Music Program," *Action, Criticism, and Theory for Music Education* 20, no. 3 (2021): 19–43; Paul Woodford, *Music Education in an Age of Virtuality and Post-truth* (New York: Routledge, 2018).

15. Cathy Benedict and Jared O'Leary, "Reconceptualizing 'Music Making': Music Technology and Freedom in the Age of Neoliberalism," *Action, Criticism, and Theory for Music Education* 18, no. 1 (2019): 26–43.

16. Joseph Abramo, "Whence Culture and Epistemology? Dialectical Materialism and Music Education," *Philosophy of Music Education Review* 29, no. 2 (2021): 155–73; Vincent Bates, "Standing at the Intersection of Race and Class in Music Education," *Action, Criticism, and Theory for Music Education* 18, no. 1 (2019): 117–60.

17. hooks, *Where We Stand*, 7.

18. Michel Foucault, *The Birth of Biopolitics*, ed. Michel Senellart, trans. Graham Burchell (New York: Palgrave Macmillan, 2008).

19. Many music education philosophers have called for attention to ethical action. See, for recent examples, Randall Allsup, *Remixing the Classroom* (Bloomington: Indiana University Press, 2016); Randall Allsup and Heidi Westerlund, "Methods and Situational Ethics in Music Education," *Action, Criticism, and Theory for Music Education* 11, no. 1 (2012): 124–48. In chapter 4, I explain how my equity-focused normative ethical approach differs from more open ethical philosophies.

20. "Inside Amazon's Employment Machine," *New York Times*, June 15, 2021, https://www.nytimes.com/interactive/2021/06/15/us/amazon-workers.html.

21. Marianna Ritchey, *Composing Capital: Classical Music in the Neoliberal Era* (Chicago: University of Chicago Press, 2019), 20.

ACKNOWLEDGMENTS

NARRATIVES ABOUT INDIVIDUALS WHO RESILIENTLY overcome adversity, achieving their main accomplishments with minimal support from others, reinforce the problematic extreme self-reliance key to contemporary capitalist societies. In contrast, I acknowledge that this book only exists because of my dependence on mentors and supportive individuals throughout my life. I am grateful for wonderful teachers of English and other subjects who challenged my writing and thinking during primary and secondary school, dedicated mentors from my undergraduate and graduate studies, and reviewers and editors from various music education journals who volunteered time to provide constructive feedback on my work. In particular, I am appreciative of the two anonymous reviewers who offered detailed, helpful comments on this manuscript. I am also grateful to the Indiana University Jacobs School of Music for providing me with a sabbatical, during which I initially conceived this book, and to my outstanding music education colleagues for fostering a positive, productive, and inspiring work environment.

The idea for this project had two sources. First, School of Education colleague Quentin Wheeler-Bell has long challenged me to consider the foundational role of class and economics in fostering inequity. Second, in fall 2020, I attended a weekly reading group run by the Indiana University Center for Theoretical Inquiry in the Humanities that focused on capitalism, a topic I knew little about. I am grateful to Cara Bernard, who provided brilliant feedback on many early drafts of chapters, as well as to students in the 2022 and 2024 Jacobs graduate Sociology of Music classes, who engaged with this work. Thanks also to Jen Blackwell and the Northwestern University students who offered insights about draft chapters and to the many colleagues who dialogued with me when I presented pieces of this project at various conferences. Fellow members of the weekly philosophy of education reading group I organize also assisted me in thinking through key texts used in this book.

This work (and play) would not have been possible without the unceasing love and support of my husband Phil. His commitment to equally parenting our energetic daughter provided me the time necessary to complete this project. Furthermore, our near daily intellectual conversations and prolonged discussions at the Dunkirk Library sharpened my ideas about the topics addressed in this book as well as my critical and creative thinking processes more broadly. I am indebted—but not in the capitalist sense—to these and many other individuals.

POPULAR MUSIC
WILL NOT SAVE US

ONE

AN INTRODUCTION TO CAPITALISM AND MUSIC EDUCATION

EXAMINING TO WHAT EXTENT MUSIC education corresponds with or challenges capitalist ideals involves understanding how capitalism functions, including its central values. Two features that distinguish capitalism from other economic systems are the private ownership of production and the aim of making a profit. Distinct from government or collective property, private property enables individuals to control certain aspects of production. In capitalist logic, an individual musician has little incentive to invest in, for example, a new piece of DJ equipment if their neighbors will have the same access to it. Alternatively, if owning the equipment enables the individual musician to charge fees for others to borrow it, then they can not only recoup their investment but also make a profit from others' labor.

While governments within capitalist systems may provide certain services and enact regulations, they rely on private production for everything from food to technological goods to musical entertainment. Capitalist producers who own the means of production pay wages to the workers—be they farmhands, computer engineers, or musicians—who create the goods. Consumers then freely purchase these goods through an open market system, and producers retain the profits, or what remains after the cost of materials and labor.

In order to facilitate transactions between individual producers and consumers, capitalism demands a monetary system. Money therefore temporarily embodies a commodity's value. For example, instead of considering how many apples one could trade for a used clarinet, apples translate directly into money, which can then be used to purchase clarinets and other goods. How much a consumer will pay for a certain product constitutes that product's exchange value. If someone pays twenty dollars for a private guitar lesson at a music store today, then that lesson is currently valued at twenty dollars. Since the same lesson might be valued at eighteen dollars or twenty-five dollars another day, the exchange value of the lesson—or any other capitalist commodity—is temporary.

CIRCULATION AND ACCUMULATION

The circulation of value through labor, commodities, and money within open, noncoercive markets constitutes a capitalist system. Stated differently, capitalist processes involve value becoming congealed in money, then into commodities, then back into money form.[1] Marxist scholar David Harvey summarizes that capitalism is best understood as an ongoing process, "specifically, the circulation of values," rather than a stagnant structure.[2]

A monetized society, however, is not necessarily a capitalist society.[3] When money serves simply to facilitate transactions between commodities, it does not produce any capital, or added value. For example, if a solo farmer sells his vegetables directly at a farmers' market for twenty dollars and then uses that twenty dollars to buy a voice lesson from an educator who teaches from home, then the money simply eases a trade of commodities; in theory, the farmer could have traded the vegetables directly for the voice lesson. This is how working class individuals, meaning anyone not in the capitalist class, typically understand and engage with money. Working-class individuals receive a wage from an employer and use that wage to buy commodities, including necessities like food and, if possible, luxury items.

In contrast, members of the capitalist class aim for the circulation of money and commodities to produce more money.[4] Harvey explains, "Capital emerges when money is put into circulation in order to get more money."[5] Capitalist-class individuals use money to buy raw materials, tools, and wage labor. From that investment, a commodity such as a musical instrument is produced. The capitalist-class producer sells the commodity for more money than they invested in the materials, tools, and labor, thus recouping their investment and producing capital as profit for themselves.

Likewise, imagine if the aforementioned voice lesson took place at a music store rather than at the educator's home. While the price of the lesson may relate to the cost of the teacher's training and expertise as well as the rent, electricity, and other expenses of running the music store, it would also include profit for the individual or company who owns the music store. As such, capitalist exchanges, which aim for profit resulting from the exchange of commodities and services, contrast situations in which money serves as an easy means of exchange between individuals (e.g., farmer directly with music teacher).

Ongoing capitalist circulation processes necessitate that capital, in the form of profits, continually increases. In Harvey's words: "Capitalism is always about growth. There can be no such thing as a capitalist social order that is not about growth and accumulation on a progressively increasing scale."[6] In pursuit of unending growth, the capitalist class strives to transcend, bypass, or circumvent all limits, including environmental, social, political, and geographical ones.[7] Capitalist practices thus exploit not only workers but also soil and other natural resources for the sake of short-term gains.[8] Stated differently, the aims of production and accumulation for their own sake—rather than to fulfill preexisting needs, social improvements, or other ends—serve as defining characteristics of capitalism.[9]

Since capitalism is an ongoing process rather than a fixed structure, it need not look the same at various times and places. While globally connected, capitalism in the United States functions differently than capitalism in more social democratic countries, such as Norway, or more authoritarian countries, such as Singapore. For example, Singapore often ranks as the most economically free country in the world, in large part because of its efficient government, zero-tariff trade agreements, and low individual and corporate tax rates.[10] Yet because the Singapore government owns 90 percent of the country's land and large shares in many prominent businesses,[11] it directly profits from free market practices. Alternatively, contemporary capitalist practices in North America, Australia, and much of Europe and South America stem directly from government nonintervention policies often grouped under the term *neoliberalism*. Examining the capitalist practices that preceded neoliberalism illuminates the uniqueness of neoliberal ideals.

A BRIEF HISTORY OF CAPITALISM

Although scholars typically date the continuous development of capitalism to the sixteenth century, pockets of capitalism arose in Europe during the late Middle Ages.[12] Writing about music and capitalism, Timothy Taylor states that in 1498, Italian printer Ottaviano Petrucci petitioned the Venetian government to protect his invention of a movable type that enabled mass printing and publishing of music, thus turning music into a commodity.[13] David Elliott and Marissa Silverman note that almost three hundred years later, around 1777, English copyright law emphasized the "score-concept" of music. This commodification of musical scores—and later, musical works more broadly—enriched publishers, who owned the rights to composers' scores, leaving composers "grossly underpaid."[14]

Early capitalist exchanges in the sixteenth and seventeenth centuries relied heavily on government investment and intervention. The rise of strong European nation-states, more uniform monetary systems, and the pillaging, exploitation, enslavement, and colonization of lands and peoples throughout the world furthered opportunities for the exchange of goods and wealth accumulation.[15] Simultaneously, the sixteenth century Protestant Reformation lessened Christian religious leaders' long-standing disdain for the acquisition of material goods while placing greater emphasis on hard work.[16] Believing that wealth resulted from hard work and that hard work was morally good, church leaders began justifying economic inequality based on wealthy individuals' virtuousness and poor individuals' supposed lack thereof.[17]

In contrast with early capitalism, classical capitalism, which scholars understand as beginning with the Industrial Revolution in 1760,[18] relies on a distinction between the natural laws of the free market and government processes. Detailed by Adam Smith in his 1776 book *The Wealth of Nations*, classical capitalism centers on the belief that governments need not intervene in the free market because humans naturally regulate supply, demand, and the competitive exchange of goods and services. In classical capitalist logic, minimization of political meddling in economic practices ensures maximum social prosperity and progress. Nobel Prize–winning economist Paul Krugman summarizes that after the publication of Smith's text, "an extensive body of economic theory was developed, whose central message was: Trust the market."[19]

Colonialization and extreme violence spread and entrenched the ideology of classical capitalism throughout much of the world. Although some Europeans were compelled to either accept wage labor or risk starvation and incarceration in debtors' prisons, Harvey explains that many Europeans "were not so much forced off the land as attracted off the land by employment possibilities and the prospects of a better life offered by urbanization and industrialization."[20] The economic benefits made possible by the influx of new labor, however, were far from equally distributed.

Urbanization often meant radical disempowerment of women as well as increased numbers of unwaged workers. While prior to the Industrial Revolution, many European women had made economic contributions through enterprises such as raising cows on local common land, urban-centered capitalist practices increasingly reduced women to the status of property.[21] Women undertook unpaid household and reproductive labor at the behest of their wage-earning husbands, on whose income they depended for survival.[22] Moreover, the completely unwaged labor of slaves and other individuals in forced working conditions furthered the capitalist maxim of making labor as cheap as possible in order to increase profits. The unwaged labor of women and enslaved persons provided industrial workers a sense of superiority amid their own dismal employment conditions. Fear that workers could fall to an even lower rung on the capitalist pyramid discouraged collective mobilization.

CAPITALISM AND MUSIC

Since profit within capitalism relies on the circulation of commodities, capitalist growth encourages the commodification of music, art, and other cultural practices. Taylor explains that during the late nineteenth and early twentieth centuries, American composers increasingly conceptualized their work in terms of exchangeability.[23] For example, aspiring songwriters like Irving Berlin flocked to Tin Pan Alley in New York with the hopes of selling their compositions to publishing houses. Rather than needing to please a single patron or local public, these composers' success—and more broadly, the profits of the publishing houses—depended on the wider popularity of their tunes.

Similarly, since music education practices often employ similar, agreed-upon resources, the more widespread they become, the more profits they create for certain individuals. At the turn of the nineteenth century, students in New England not only paid a fee to attend private singing schools but were also required to purchase books created by singing masters.[24] The more students enrolled, the more singing masters profited from both tuition fees and book sales. Lowell Mason, who played a key role in establishing music education as a regular part of American public school curricula, profited handsomely from sales of his pedagogical publications and other associated business ventures.[25]

Although key contemporary music groups—including the International Society for Music Education (ISME), the American National Association for Music Education (NAfME), and the popular music–education group Music Will—are nonprofit organizations, they financially benefit from sponsorship by wealthy corporations and, in turn, promote positive images of these businesses. ISME established music education advocacy awards sponsored by Parsons Music of Hong Kong,[26] "one of the world's top three piano manufacturers, seventh largest world retailer and China's number one musical instrument retailer."[27] NAfME receives funding from companies ranging from Alfred Music to Quaver Ed to Yamaha,[28] while Music Will's website currently lists sixteen corporate partners, including Bloomberg, Goldman Sachs, Mattel, NASDAQ, and Zildjian.[29]

The commodification of music and expansion of profit-based music businesses in the early twentieth century attracted the notice of prominent critics. Offering a stinging assessment of the culture industry, Theodore Adorno understood popular music, including jazz, as fostering a passivity that inhibited attention to one's economic condition. Adorno argued that by equating continual sameness with progress, the culture industry provided "fleeting gratification" while reinforcing "shamelessly conformist" behavior patterns.[30] Similarly, he asserted that listening to familiar pieces of classical music, such as popular Beethoven sonatas, encouraged passivity and hence continuation of current practices, including economic exploitation.[31]

Adorno had little hope that artistic practices could fundamentally challenge problematic aspects of twentieth-century capitalism. Musicologist Marianna Ritchey summarizes: "Adorno sees capitalism as a totalizing system of dehumanizing oppression, and holds that the best music can hope for is to tell the truth about this condition by embodying our own alienation and reflecting it back to us."[32] Specifically referencing the atonal music of Alban Berg and Arnold Schoenberg, Adorno proposed that engagement with nonpopular music can awaken reflection on one's economic realities.[33] He believed that the jarring unexpectedness of atonal music making incites a momentary disruption that may cause listeners to question their socioeconomic positionality.[34]

More recently, Jacques Attali, in his 1977 book *Noise: The Political Economy of Music*, proposed that composing music enables freedom from repetitive music making that parallels and furthers the confines of capitalism. In Attali's view, composing should involve making music outside of the accumulation of capitalist value.[35] Specifically, this act can involve calling into question the division between worker (composer) and consumer (listener) by reimagining listening as rewriting and hence, in a way, composing.[36] Stated differently, treating listening as an act of creation as opposed to one of consumption troubles predetermined capitalist worker-consumer relations.

While many of Adorno's and Attali's critiques remain relevant for contemporary music industry practices, they wrote during time periods when there still existed a degree of tension between governments and free market economic practices.[37] For example, following the Great Depression in the United States in the 1930s, President Franklin D. Roosevelt and other government leaders advanced economic policies that limited and regulated free markets. Although schooling had always necessitated a consumption of resources, such as textbooks and musical instruments, that benefited capitalist producers, primary and secondary public schools were somewhat insulated from free market practices during this period. The fact that disparities based on class, gender, and race persisted and even flourished within education and other public spheres at this time reveals that the tension between government regulation and free market forces left many serious social issues unresolved. Yet today's governments' adoption of neoliberal policies has worsened global economic inequality.

THE NEOLIBERAL TURN

Since the 1970s, both conservative and liberal leaders throughout the world have embraced neoliberal policies and practices.[38] Neoliberals and liberals alike emphasize government noninterventionism in markets. José Luis Aróstegui explains neoliberalism as "purely economic," its influence on society resulting from its economic rationale "rather than due to an elaboration of a theory of civil rights."[39] In contrast with neoliberals, classical liberals maintain an emphasis on the government's role in addressing societal issues and democratic engagement.

Classical capitalism seeks to separate government work and free market practices, but neoliberal proponents turn this distinction into a hierarchy, with the government becoming subservient to the free market. Stated differently, the neoliberal economic movement emphasizes the supremacy of the free market. In political theorist Wendy Brown's words, the term *neoliberalism* is "associated with a bundle of policies privatizing public ownership and services, radically reducing the social state, leashing labor, deregulating capital, and producing a tax-and- tariff-friendly climate to direct foreign investors."[40] While proponents of classical capitalism aim to avoid government interference in the free market, proponents of neoliberal capitalism desire to minimize government spending and social intervention altogether.

Since proponents of neoliberalism aim to limit the spending and influence of public authorities, neoliberal governments increasingly outsource services they once provided—ranging from schooling to outer space exploration—to the free market.[41] For example, consider the American school choice movement. Rather than requiring students to attend the public school located closest to their place of residence, parents in some states can use school choice programs to receive a voucher toward a private school or opt into a different public school, including publicly funded charter schools. School choice policies rest on the idea that when parent consumers select the best performing schools, market competition will either improve or eliminate the less desirable ones.[42]

Through such neoliberal policies and actions, market principles become governing principles. When schools, including private schools, compete to attract student-customers, they enable corporations to profit from taxpayer dollars. This system incentivizes corporations to fund political candidates who support neoliberal policies, thus further limiting the government's ability to address problematic aspects and outcomes of free market practices, including growing economic disparities. For example, exclusionary tactics (e.g., not adequately serving students with special needs) and differential access to information and resources (e.g., parent transportation) mean that neoliberal school choice policies further segregate students along race and other lines,[43] ultimately exacerbating socioeconomic inequities.

The advent of significant neoliberal policies in the United States coincided with changing attitudes about poverty. Neoliberal proponents furthered the idea that anyone could attain riches through hard work and inventive thinking.[44] Major religious organizations increasingly shifted from understanding individuals in poverty as deserving assistance to blaming them for their plight.[45] In bell hooks's words, "suddenly notions of communalism were replaced with notions of self-interest."[46] Before considering how self-interest informs the identities of individuals in contemporary capitalist societies, I examine the place-based nature of neoliberalism and provide an overview of music education scholars' investigations of neoliberalism.

Though a widely adapted ideological system, neoliberalism has local variants.[47] As such, my own place-based experiences and positionality as a member of the United States professional managerial class inform how I interpret and engage with neoliberal theories and critiques, as well as with contemporary capitalism more broadly. Although I at points aim to think alongside scholars from regions beyond Europe and North America, my overall reliance on Western philosophy and ways of knowing is a limitation of this text.

Yet there are advantages to examining neoliberalism from an American-centric perspective. Explaining her focus on the United States in *Composing Capital: Classical Music in the Neoliberal Era* as a conscious choice, Ritchey notes that neoliberalism originated in the United States, elaborating that "its global spread is widely seen as an outsourcing of American prerogatives."[48] Furthermore, Krugman argues that America exemplifies how decades of minimally regulated capitalist practices build an ever-solidifying pyramid of economic winners and losers.[49] Examining neoliberal policies and contemporary capitalist practices within the context of the United States may therefore provide insights about how such ideas continue to impact other nations as they flow through globally connected societies.

NEOLIBERALISM AND MUSIC EDUCATION: WINNERS, LOSERS, AND MARCHING BAND TROPHIES

Music education scholars have explained how teachers and students both experience the effects of neoliberal policies and enact practices that reinforce neoliberal ideals. Music educators have documented the adverse effects of neoliberal policies of centralization, standardization, and efficiency on music education practices in Australia, Europe, North America, and South America.[50]

For example, Martin Fautley describes how policymakers in England created target achievement scores associated with the standardized national curriculum. As the scores became the primary goal of education, assessment switched from a process of monitoring pupils' growth "to a process of monitoring teaching via grades."[51] Paul Woodford notes that neoliberal policies have made both school principals and higher education leaders increasingly accountable to politicians and educational bureaucrats.[52] Moreover, Aróstegui explains that the neoliberal emphasis on quantifiable outcomes in language arts, mathematics, and science classes have caused Spanish education leaders to question the presence of music and arts within schools.[53]

Music educators, including policymakers, have also directly contributed to neoliberal standardization efforts. Jess Mullen argues that the neoliberal orientation of contemporary music standards undermines music educators' claim to center music understanding and making for all.[54] He explains that "by linking music education to workplace skills, establishing uniform benchmarks to improve educational efficiency, and codifying long held Eurocentric epistemologies of musical value, the National Core Arts Standards in Music stand to exacerbate existing inequities in music classrooms."[55] Although Paul Louth notes that increased emphasis on standards and state-wide testing works in tension with other neoliberal ideals, such as nonintervention and decentralization,[56] the ongoing measurement and accountability both foisted on and enacted by music educators reinforces the efficiency-based, free market supremacy promoted by neoliberal policy advocates.

Neoliberal emphasis on standardization and accountability works in tandem with competitive dispositions. Sean Powell argues that "under a one-dimensional neoliberal educational regime," music teaching and learning based on competitive performance practices reinforce the idea that society is and should be stratified according to standardized, quantitative measures, thus limiting possibilities for creativity and personal development.[57] More broadly, capitalist emphasis on continual competition has led to international comparisons of education outcomes.[58] Examining educational statements posted on various government websites, Cathy Benedict concludes that these documents use discourses "originally intended to speak for oppressed populations" to propose "the goal of education in terms of global markets and competition."[59]

More specifically, Vincent Bates posits that understanding large ensemble performance as the ultimate, bottom-line goal of K-12 music education foregrounds efficient pedagogy and the interests of economically privileged suburban districts.[60] Given that music programs and individual students do not have equal access to private instruction, music competitions further existing socioeconomic hierarchies, often under the guise of being meritocratic.[61] Stated differently, advocating that music education is "for all" works in tension with exclusionary competitive practices.[62] Although competition can serve as a form of self-fulfilling play,[63] widespread, high-stakes music competition practices typically undermine such possibilities.

Taken together, standardization, accountability, and competition facilitate education practices that benefit capitalist producers.[64] These pervasive economic-centered rationalities influence and limit what educators understand as normal, desirable, and even possible.[65] Writing about neoliberalism within higher education, Woodford summarizes: "Administration and also many colleagues portray this brave new world as only natural, right, and true rather than as a political imposition."[66] In short, contemporary economic practices influence not only the actions of students and teachers but also their self-conceptions.

THE CAPITALIST SUBJECT

When governments become subservient to free market practices, individuals have increased incentives to focus their self-conception on qualities that serve their personal economic interests. As such, one's identity as a member of various civic communities may become secondary to their identity as a capitalist worker and consumer. In Michel Foucault's words, neoliberalism demands the redefinition of the subject as an entrepreneur of the self.[67] Likewise, contemporary feminist scholar Angela McRobbie notes that "few aspects of everyday life and working life are now exempt from this requirement to self-promote."[68] Even those wishing to take part in public debate against neoliberal ills must find entertaining ways of making their voices visible on social media.[69]

Individuals living in contemporary capitalist societies can build their self-brands through not only long-standing social markers, such as clothing and cultural tastes, but also content they continually post on social media and virtual support or disdain for others' content, including musical endeavors. Explaining this self-branding as a form of hyperindividualism, Taylor notes that people often fashion and continually refine their identities through their music choices.[70] In such moments, selecting favorite tunes becomes less about identifying with a wider group of like-minded music makers and more about setting oneself apart as a unique individual who successfully competes for followers, social standing, and financial opportunities.

Although I have focused on neoliberalism thus far, I refer to capitalism for the remainder of this text. Contemporary capitalist practices are largely a continuation of neoliberal initiatives that began in the 1970s. Yet, as suggested by the title of Brown's 2018 book *In the Ruins of Neoliberalism: The Rise of Antidemocratic Politics in the West,* enough time has passed that individuals and societies have felt and reacted to the compounding effects of neoliberal policies. For example, neoliberal deregulation of the banking industry enabled the 2007 worldwide financial crisis, which in turn led to government intervention to stop major financial institutions from failing.

Since government intervention is antithetical to neoliberal ideals, such action evidences that contemporary capitalist practices have incorporated and moved beyond neoliberalism. In the words of *New Yorker* author Andrew Marantz, "it's reasonable to wonder whether Biden will be the last President of the neoliberal era, or the first President of whatever comes next."[71] Throughout this text, I use the term *capitalism* in reference to contemporary globalized capitalist practices. My observations and critiques do not necessarily apply to capitalist systems heavily regulated by governments capable of making and enforcing policies that, for example, stop and reverse wealth concentration and global warming.

CAPITALIST SUBJECTS AND MUSIC EDUCATION

Music educators have examined how contemporary capitalist ideals may parallel or inform self-making within teaching and learning settings. Benedict argues that teachers often enact Orff and Kodály practices in unmindful ways that treat music making as a commodity.[72] Like a capitalist worker producing a specific product, such music educators use solfège and hand signs toward a functional, predetermined musical end, omitting or minimizing potential creative uses of music making.[73] She elaborates: "The teachers, who presume to own the mode of production, are in reality alienated from the educative process as they are, in reality, handmaidens to a discourse of normative and commonsense social production of what counts as knowledge and unfortunately, in many cases, what counts as music."[74] Stated differently, music educators who work to produce the product of hand sign–centered music literacy take on capitalist worker identities disconnected from the spontaneous joy of contextually specific, imaginative musical experiences.

Making a related argument about secondary school music ensembles, Joseph Abramo compares the hiding of labor within capitalist commodities to refined ensemble competition performances that conceal the labor involved in music learning.[75] Just as a laptop computer displayed in a pristine store conceals the dangerous process of mining rare minerals and other laborious tasks that enabled its production, performers present polished shows that hide the hard work of developing musical skills. The sleeker the laptop, the higher the price; likewise, the more seemingly effortless the performance, the higher the score from the judges.[76] Music ensemble participants internalize a capitalist consumer identity in which they focus on the measured exchange value, indicated by the judges' score, rather than the labor—in this case, the learning processes—enabling the creation of the performance and resulting score. This action parallels consumers who focus on the price of a laptop or other commodity but omit attention to the labor that produced it.

More recently, Abramo has examined how the capitalist process of dematerialization, or moving from concrete commodities (e.g., compact discs) to more fluid ones (e.g., music streaming services), parallels changes in conceptions underlying music education sociological research.[77] He describes that music educators privilege symbols and abstract notions of culture (e.g., performing music from diverse composers) over material realities (e.g., talking about wealth inequality). While performing music from diverse composers creates a meaningful break from long-standing exclusionary practices, such action does not expose, let alone address, the material inequities on which contemporary capitalism depends.

In summary, music educators and students might understand capitalism not just as an economic system in which people participate but also as a set of guiding values that fundamentally interface with and shape humans' individual and collective identities. This identity formation influences engagements with cultural practices, including music making. In Taylor's words: "Without capitalism, after all, most of what we think about music wouldn't be possible. . . . Capitalism powerfully shaped not only the production, consumption, and distribution of music but also the roles that music plays in people's lives."[78] Yet Taylor also observes that theories about how capitalism shapes culture remain rare.[79] So why might music educators care about their role in creating and reinforcing capitalist subjects?

PROBLEMS OF CONTEMPORARY GLOBALIZED CAPITALISM

One significant result of capitalist emphasis on individual self-branding and competition is the undermining of social responsibility. If one's identity within a capitalist society centers on their individual consumption practices, then they have less energy for attending to social concerns or inequities in the production-consumption process. In Aróstegui's words: "The application of economic criteria to education . . . outlines a type of person, the homo oeconomicus, which is individualistic and asocial."[80]

Going further, Brown asserts that individualism is not a byproduct of capitalist competition but a key part of the contemporary capitalist project.[81] Since exploited individuals could work together to secure more equitable conditions for themselves, proponents of contemporary capitalist practices understand "shoring up individuals and families against the forces of capitalism that threaten them" as a central aim.[82] When workers experiencing turmoil look to themselves and their families as their primary form of support, they avoid the use of government resources. This imposed self-reliance enables governments to become smaller and interfere less with capitalist production practices, which often results in greater profits for the capitalist class. Since civic institutions provide communal voice and material support for exploited workers, Brown summarizes that proponents of an unbridled free market understand "negating the very idea of the social" as key.[83]

A related second outcome of contemporary capitalist practices is that, in the absence of collectively negotiated ethics, maximizing economic growth can become synonymous with ethical action. As Harvard ethics professor Michael Sandel explains, individuals may presume that those who have the most money have contributed the most to the common good by producing products and services consumers value.[84] Since such thinking makes wealth an unquestioned indicator of one's virtuousness, the most profitable capitalist producers become role models worthy of emulation. This world view leaves the roles of inherited privilege, unfair or illegal business practices, and other potentially problematic qualities and actions unacknowledged and unquestioned.

Moreover, capitalism proponents argue that because the extraction of resources by wealthy countries from less wealthy ones creates economic growth, such action is ethical.[85] Through this reasoning, scenarios in which workers receive meager wages laboring in dangerous conditions while the capitalist class retains most of the profit do not undermine the fundamental ethical nature of such enterprises. Argentinian scholar Verónica Gago summarizes: "According to this perspective, anyone who opposes the extractive model is opposed to a form of financing poor populations."[86] Such thinking understands market gains as unquestionably ethical, leaving issues related to the human exploitation and natural resource decimation that enable capitalist growth unconsidered.

A third problematic result of the market becoming a substitute for ethical considerations is that societies accept drastic wealth inequalities as normal, inevitable, or even beneficial. In Ritchey's words: "The principal tenet of modern capitalism is that those with capital must try to accumulate more. . . . Whether or not all individuals have the legal right to better their own personal position within this system via hard work or luck does not change the basic inequality on which the system functions."[87] Although current capitalist systems provide few opportunities for social mobility, the aim of unceasing wealth accumulation necessitates that even completely meritocratic capitalist practices result in pyramidal resource distribution, with a few rich individuals at the top and the masses struggling financially below.

Even if one willingly accepts the inequalities inherent in capitalism, those differences have increased to monumental proportions. In the United States, there is little debate that income inequality has grown markedly since the 1970s,[88] and Harvey observes that staggering levels of social inequality have developed in other countries with significant neoliberal policies.[89] Furthermore, authors of a Credit Suisse report on global wealth have found that while the richest 1 percent of the world's population own 43.4 percent of all wealth, 53.6 percent of the population (adults with less than $10,000 USD in wealth) own a total of 1.4 percent.[90]

This growing economic inequality has social and environmental impacts, including increased political polarization. Writing about the expanding worker-CEO wealth divide, Krugman explains: "Not only did it mean that ordinary families were failing to share in economic progress, it meant a loss of our sense of living in a shared society."[91] As demonstrated during the 2020 COVID-19 pandemic, wealthy individuals could seclude themselves for months on yachts and in island mansions while many of those at the bottom of the capitalist pyramid died providing essential food, goods, and services to the general population.

More broadly, savage global inequalities create political instability, leading to refugees and ultimately a "surplus humanity" that cannot be easily incorporated into the global capitalist system.[92] Refugees to Europe and the United States come in large part because global extraction practices have stolen material riches from Africa and South America while destabilizing and devastating local political and cultural practices, creating desperate situations ripe for violence and corruption. Governments aim to control this population by sealing it out, building border walls, and creating mass incarceration systems.[93] Furthermore, the ongoing extraction and depletion of the earth's resources in the name of profit and consumerist pleasure have significantly contributed to global warming and created more hazardous circumstances for the marginalized persons most likely to suffer from human-influenced natural catastrophes such as rising sea levels and wildfires.

Relatedly, racial divides are key to the functioning of capitalist systems. Zeus Leonardo argues that racism is not just a byproduct of late global capitalism but a key enabling factor.[94] He writes that "the greater concentration of people of color within the lower ranks of the division of labor, the material deprivations of ghettoization and general housing segregation, and the preparation of students in an equally segregated schooling experience all point to the internal dynamics of capitalism. . . . Racist behaviors and policies produce economic outcomes because racism strengthens and complements capitalism."[95] As long as capitalism exists, there will be economic winners and losers; as long as there are winners and losers, individuals—particularly those lower on but not at the bottom of the economic pyramid—will attempt to keep Black individuals, as well as other racial and ethnic minorities, from advancing their economic standing. While there remain aspects of contemporary racism for which a socioeconomic-focused class analysis cannot account,[96] examining racism absent attention to current economic practices is unlikely to provide significant material benefits to Black, Brown, Indigenous, and Asian individuals.[97] White workers continue clinging to whiteness "because in some fundamental sense it is all they have."[98]

Like race, gender plays a key role in maintaining capitalist hierarchies. Silvia Federici explains that women's unpaid and underpaid labor enhances profits for the capitalist class while exposing women to sexual harassment and abuse.[99] She describes: "If women earned higher wages, if waitresses did not depend on tips to pay the rent, if film directors and producers couldn't decide the future of young women who turn to them for jobs, if we could leave abusive relationships or jobs in which we are sexually harassed—then we would see a change."[100]

More broadly, proponents of unrestrained capitalism have adopted and adapted aspects of feminism to dismantle government welfare programs. McRobbie describes how, as exemplified by books like Sheryl Sandberg's *Lean In: Women, Work, and the Will to Lead*, self-described feminist authors promote an exhausting balance of work and career rather than advocating for changes to working conditions and gender equality.[101] When "banal phrases like the 'work-life balance' come to replace more sustained debate about how motherhood and work could realistically be combined," individuals must compromise at work and rely on spouses, reinforcing gender traditionalism in order to meet dual roles as workers and parents.[102] In short, educating individuals about systemic gender injustices without attending to economic motivators and beneficiaries of said inequities may have minimal impact on material circumstances.

ROLE OF MUSIC EDUCATION

In addition to promoting standardization, accountability, and competitive dispositions that benefit capitalist producers, music education practices often emphasize the capitalist ideal of unrestrained growth. Many contemporary music educators treat growth in the form of ever-advancing competition scores as unquestionably good. Powell notes that "the demand for perpetual growth in performance achievement mirrors exactly neoliberal capitalism's requirement for perpetual economic growth."[103] Although marching band competition scores tend to correlate positively with schools' socioeconomic profiles,[104] many competitively unsuccessful teachers maintain that hard work can enable them to reap the system's rewards.[105] Amid experiencing perpetual disappointment, they reinforce the myth that music education—and by extension, society more broadly—is fundamentally meritocratic. Yet teachers and students who achieve desired competitive goals do not necessarily experience satisfaction. As Powell notes, just as capitalist consumers never can never buy enough, achieving a long-sought musical goal only creates the desire to compete harder and achieve bigger goals.[106]

Music education philosophers have also detailed how seemingly progressive music education content and practices can further capitalist ills. Gareth Dylan Smith explains how successful female popular musicians often reinforce masculine domination. He argues that Beyoncé Knowles's achievement "is entirely consistent with the gender roles permitted in the music industry—women (especially the most physically attractive ones) have always been allowed to front bands in mainstream popular music, as this fits the stereotype expected in a hetero-normative patriarchal structure."[107] Alternatively, Cathy Benedict and Jared O'Leary explain that music educators' use of certain technologies can advance dominant commercial interests while subordinating students' creative music making.[108]

Expanding on this logic, Abramo illuminates the relationship between capitalism and popular culture more broadly. If capitalism creates culture, Abramo argues, then music education practices and critiques that begin in culture, such as those related to culturally relevant pedagogy, cannot adequately challenge capitalist ways of knowing.[109] Since the music a student listens to outside of school arises from and is sustained through capitalist exchanges, teaching such music in school does little to change material inequities resulting from capitalism.

Given that contemporary capitalist practices rely on gender, racial, and other hierarchies, it follows that when music educators reinforce students' identities as capitalist consumers and promote values that benefit capitalist producers, they indirectly reinforce such inequities. Yet examinations of how innovative music education practices and associated values might reinforce capitalist ills are rare. Before further investigating how contemporary music education practices correspond with key capitalist values in chapter 2, I provide a few points of clarification.

MARX AND THE S-WORD

Scholarly writers who address capitalism necessarily engage with Karl Marx's writings about capital. Many people associate Marx with his *Communist Manifesto,* which promotes a template for a new economic order. Alternatively, in *Das Kapital,* Marx aims to provide a scientific understanding of capitalism by focusing on observations about capitalist processes. Marx points out problems of capitalism and makes predictions about what could happen to capitalist systems but offers few demands for changed action.[110] Given that the progression of capitalism since Marx's time makes much of *Das Kapital* outdated, I draw largely on contemporary Marx-inspired scholars, including Brown and Harvey.[111] However, Harvey notes that neoliberal policies have in part globally reconstituted the vastly inequitable economic conditions Marx described in the 1850s and 1860s, making parts of *Das Kapital* relevant for interrogating contemporary capitalism.[112] To avoid reinscribing Marx's straight, white, European, male worldview, I complement his work with writings from contemporary female perspectives on capitalism, including Brown's and Fraser's, as well as work from queer and Indigenous scholars, including Sara Ahmed, Donna Haraway, and Dylan Robinson.

While this text offers a significant critique of capitalism, I find it important to recognize salient arguments made by its proponents. Wealthy individuals have provided significant support for causes that benefit humanity, including artistic endeavors. For example, billionaire David H. Koch funded the building of a theater at Lincoln Center, and Warren Buffett has pledged that charities will receive roughly 99 percent of his estimated $120 billion fortune.[113]

Furthermore, capitalist practices are in part responsible for raising the overall global standard of living and life expectancy. More humans have access to plentiful food, clean water, and education than at any other time in history. Although this achievement does not excuse the racism, sexism, cultural hegemony, human exploitation, resource depletion, and material inequalities that enable these advances, it is simplistic to dismiss capitalism as unequivocally bad.

It is equally problematic to understand capitalism as inherently good. Music educators, and indeed all members of capitalist societies, have an obligation to acknowledge the serious limitations of contemporary globalized capitalist practices. For example, it is extremely troubling that the total wealth of sixty-two individuals equals that of the planet's poorest 3.5 billion (half of all humanity).[114] Krugman, a procapitalist economist, bemoans that defenders of capitalism use phrases like "Marxist talk" to dissuade "even bringing up the distribution of income, or comparing the growth in middle-class incomes with those of the rich."[115] Considering issues of inequity and wealth distribution is not the same as advocating for the loaded s-word: socialism.

Unfortunately, many politicians have furthered inaccurate use of the term *socialism*. Socialism refers to situations in which an entire community—rather than individuals—owns or regulates the means of production and exchange. In other words, capitalism, which involves private ownership of production, distribution, and exchange, is a fundamentally different economic-political arrangement than socialism, which involves communal ownership. Although few, if any, American political candidates advocate for complete socialism, conservatives have wielded the term as an insult for leftist individuals and groups, and some liberals have taken to calling themselves socialists. As Krugman explains, American politicians often conflate socialism "with what Europeans call 'social democracy'—a market economy, but with a strong public social safety net and regulations that limit the range of actions businesses can take in pursuit of profit."[116] Social democracy is a form of capitalism, but unlike the minimally regulated capitalism in the United States and elsewhere, it involves significant government regulation paired with substantial government-provided services. Given that this text focuses on identity development and action within capitalist societies as they currently exist, I rarely use the term *socialism*. Yet it is crucial that music educators understand the distinction between the ideas of capitalism, social democracy, and socialism.

While I draw on Marx's explanations and critiques of capitalism, I do not propose that the United States or any other country become communist. Marx used the terms *socialism* and *communism* interchangeably.[117] Communism, which involves common ownership of production processes and individuals working and receiving in accordance with their needs and abilities, has many theoretical and practical limitations. In this text, I neither draw on nor engage with Marx's *Communist Manifesto*.

Contemporary philosophers such as Alain Badiou and Chantel Mouffe have argued that a reimagined, communally constructed communism, rather than the top-down communism currently present in China and elsewhere, holds much promise for today's societies.[118] While I am partly sympathetic to these arguments, I find their present theorizing underdeveloped. For example, Harvey observes that because societies currently understand success in terms of economic growth, even a well-functioning communist state could not compete by this metric with its capitalist neighbors.[119] Any theorizing about a viable communist community would thus need to account for how its members would interface—or not—with global capitalism. Although I have chosen not to advocate for a variation of communism as a particularly promising way forward, I do not wish to discount such possibilities.

Neglecting to imagine socioeconomic alternatives, including imperfect ones, only furthers the narrative that capitalism is natural, unalterable, and ethically good. Since the inception of capitalism, individuals and groups have contested its values and practices. Federici argues that to assume the past or present inevitability of capitalist development "is to place ourselves on the other side of people's struggles to resist it."[120] Although music educators cannot necessarily escape or negate contemporary capitalist practices, they can consider how and to what extent they reinforce and perhaps challenge them.

Additionally, it is worth noting that Marx understands class as a binary, with a capitalist (bourgeoisie) class and a working (proletariat) class. While such a distinction is at times helpful, music making and other cultural practices often divide along more complex lines. For example, while anyone who does not own the means of production belongs to Marx's working class, Anna Bull demonstrates that middle versus lower working-class individuals often possess substantially different music tastes and other forms of cultural capital.[121] As such, I sometimes contrast the capitalist and working classes directly and at other times understand class as a continuum between lower, middle, and upper socioeconomic classes.

Marx largely understands power as a possession that some have and others lack; the capitalist class has power while the working class lacks it. I understand power in the Foucauldian sense, as circulating among individuals and in part constituting those individuals.[122] For example, a misbehaving student may hold the power to derail music making until a teacher reasserts their power by surveilling and perhaps disciplining the student. Likewise, the young adults who handcuffed themselves to a conductor's podium during a symphony orchestra concert in order to highlight the climate crisis momentarily wrested power from the more financially well-off musicians and audience members.[123]

By focusing on the circulation of power, Foucault omits the inequitable material circumstances and potential for social cohesion that Marx emphasizes. A Foucauldian awareness of power, including in relation to the role of discourse in self-construction, will not necessarily lead to the redistribution of material resources. In this text, my arguments most closely align with those of scholars such as Brown, who think at the crossroads of Foucault's and Marx's philosophies.

Both Foucault and Marx tend to treat the entrepreneurial subject as singular and universal. Alternatively, Federici argues that the contrasting racial and gender hierarchies that have enabled and furthered capitalism since its inception rule out the possibility of a singular standpoint.[124] In agreement with Federici, I understand critiques of capitalism as operating differently for those with contrasting identities and histories. Throughout this text, I address the specific impacts of capitalism on historically marginalized groups; I also acknowledge that I inevitably understand capitalism through the lens of an educationally privileged, white, able-bodied female.

Music educators and students currently reside within globalized capitalist systems that in part constitute their (entrepreneurial) self-formation. Although they cannot fully escape this aspect of their identities, they can critically position themselves in relation to contemporary capitalist practices. Socioeconomic positionalities can include thriving within, surviving under, resisting, and challenging capitalism. Within each positionality, music educators and students might consider how to address key unethical aspects of capitalism. Before arguing for specific ethical aims and describing possible socioeconomic-ethical positionalities, I examine additional intersections between contemporary capitalist ideals and current music education practices.

NOTES

1. David Harvey, *A Companion to Marx's Capital: The Complete Edition* (Brooklyn: Verso Books, 2018), 90.
2. Harvey, *Companion to Marx's Capital*, 90.
3. Harvey, *Companion to Marx's Capital*, 78.
4. Marx uses the word *bourgeoisie* when referencing the capitalist class, meaning those who own the means of production. The term *bourgeoisie* tends to invoke images of well-dressed bankers and lawyers; I find the term *capitalist class* more appropriate for a contemporary global elite that includes tech billionaires wearing jeans and T-shirts. Karl Marx, *Capital Vol. 1*, trans. Ben Fowkes (New York: Penguin, 2004).
5. Harvey, *Companion to Marx's Capital*, 78.
6. Harvey, *Companion to Marx's Capital*, 261.
7. Harvey, *Companion to Marx's Capital*, 264.
8. Marx, *Capital Vol. 1*, 638.
9. Harvey, *Companion to Marx's Capital*, 261.
10. "2021 Index of Economic Freedom," *Heritage Foundation*, 2021, https://www.heritage.org/index/ranking.

11. Matt Brueing, "How Capitalist Is Singapore Really?" *People's Policy Project*, March 9, 2018, https://www.peoplespolicyproject.org/2018/03/09/how-capitalist-is-singapore-really/.

12. R. L. Heilbroner and P. J. Boettke, "Capitalism," *Encyclopedia Britannica*, September 23, 2020, https://www.britannica.com/topic/capitalism.

13. Timothy Taylor, *Music and Capitalism: A History of the Present* (Chicago: University of Chicago Press, 2016), 22.

14. David J. Elliott and Marissa Silverman, *Music Matters: A Philosophy of Music Education* (New York: Oxford University Press, 2015), 69–70.

15. Raj Patel and Jason W. Moore, *A History of the World in Seven Cheap Things: A Guide to Capitalism, Nature, and the Future of the Planet* (Oakland: University of California Press, 2018).

16. Heilbroner and Boettke, "Capitalism."

17. Heilbroner and Boettke, "Capitalism."

18. Heilbroner and Boettke, "Capitalism."

19. Paul Krugman, *Arguing with Zombies* (New York: W. W. Norton, 2021), 132.

20. Harvey, *Companion to Marx's Capital*, 307.

21. Silvia Federici, *Patriarchy of the Wage: Notes on Marx, Gender, and Feminism* (Brooklyn: PM Press, 2021).

22. Federici, *Patriarchy of the Wage*.

23. Taylor, *Music and Capitalism*, 30.

24. Michael L. Mark and Charles L. Gary, *A History of American Music Education*, 3rd ed. (Lanham, MD: Rowman & Littlefield Education, 2007), 80.

25. Mark and Gary, *History of American Music Education*, 132.

26. See https://www.isme.org/parsons-music-advocacy-awards-brought-you-isme.

27. "Company Profile and Achievements," Parsons Music, accessed February 17, 2024, https://parsonsmusic.com.au/pages/company-profile-and-achievements.

28. "What Is the Music Education Policy Roundtable?" National Association for Music Education, accessed February 17, 2014, https://nafme.org/advocacy/policy-priorities/music-education-policy-roundtable/.

29. "Current Music Will Partners," Music Will, accessed February 17, 2024, https://current.musicwill.org/donors.

30. Theodor Adorno, *The Culture Industry: Selected Essays on Mass Culture*, ed. J. M. Bernstein (New York: Routledge, 1991), 103.

31. Theodor Adorno, *Aesthetic Theory*, trans. Robert Hullot-Kentor (Minneapolis: University of Minnesota Press, 1997).

32. Marianna Ritchey, *Composing Capital: Classical Music in the Neoliberal Era* (Chicago: University of Chicago Press, 2019), 10.

33. Adorno, *Aesthetic Theory*.

34. Adorno, *Aesthetic Theory*.

35. Jacques Attali, *Noise: The Political Economy of Music*, trans. Brian Massumi (Minneapolis: University of Minnesota Press, 1985), 135.

36. Attali, *Noise*, 135.

37. The neoliberal turn occurred in the 1970s, and Attali's aforementioned book was published in 1977. However, his descriptions primarily rely on a Marxist analysis of capitalism and make little mention of neoliberal changes that were occurring at the time of publication.

38. Wendy Brown, *In the Ruins of Neoliberalism: The Rise of Antidemocratic Politics in the West* (New York: Columbia University Press, 2018).

39. José Luis Aróstegui, "Implications of Neoliberalism and Knowledge Economy for Music Education," *Music Education Research* 22, no. 1 (2020): 44.

40. Brown, *In the Ruins of Neoliberalism*, 18.

41. Elliott and Silverman, *Music Matters*, 118.

42. See, for example, Jess Mullen, "Music Education for Some: Music Standards at the Nexus of Neoliberal Reforms and Neoconservative Values," *Action Criticism, and Theory for Music Education* 18, no. 1 (2019): 44–67.

43. Tomás Monarrez, Brian Kisida, and Matthew Chingos, "Charter School Effects on School Segregation," *Urban Institute*, July 24, 2019, https://www.urban.org/research/publication/charter-school-effects-school-segregation.

44. bell hooks, *Where We Stand: Class Matters* (New York: Routledge, 2000), 44.

45. hooks, *Where We Stand*, 44.

46. hooks, *Where We Stand*, 44.

47. Taylor, *Music and Capitalism*, 5.

48. Ritchey, *Composing Capital*, 18.

49. Krugman, *Arguing with Zombies*, 285.

50. Rolando Angel-Alvarado, Bayron Gárate-González, and Isabel Quiroga-Fuentes, "Insurrection in Chile: The Effects of Neoliberalism from a Music Education Perspective," *Action, Criticism, and Theory for Music Education* 20, no. 3 (2021): 108–31; Aróstegui, "Implications of Neoliberalism"; Martin Fautley, "Assessment Policy and Practice in Secondary Schools in the English National Curriculum," in *The Oxford Handbook of Assessment Policy and Practice in Music Education, Volume 1* (New York: Oxford University Press, 2019); Graham McPhail and Jeff McNeill, "Music Education and the Neoliberal Turn in Aotearoa New Zealand," *Action, Criticism, and Theory for Music Education* 20, no. 3 (2021): 44–81.

51. Fautley, "Assessment Policy and Practice," 228.

52. Paul Woodford, *Music Education in an Age of Virtuality and Post-truth* (New York: Routledge, 2018), 72.

53. Aróstegui, "Implications of Neoliberalism," 47.

54. Mullen, "Music Education for Some."
55. Mullen, "Music Education for Some," 44.
56. J. Paul Louth, "Emphasis and Suggestion versus Musical Taxidermy: Neoliberal Contradictions, Music Education, and the Knowledge Economy," *Philosophy of Music Education Review* 28, no. 2 (2020): 88–107.
57. Sean Robert Powell, "Competition, Ideology, and the One-Dimensional Music Program," *Action, Criticism, and Theory for Music Education* 20, no. 3 (2021): 19.
58. Cathy Benedict, "Capitalist Rationality: Comparing the Lure of the Infinite," *Philosophy of Music Education Review* 21, no. 1 (2013): 8–22. Almost a decade prior, Richard Colwell made a similar connection, noting that "globalization is synonymous with a marketplace philosophy . . . with competitors throughout the world." Richard Colwell, "A Peek at an International Perspective on Assessment," in *Music Education Entering the 21st century*, ed. Patricia Martin Shand (Western Australia: International Society for Music Education, 2004), 18.
59. Benedict, "Capitalist Rationality," 8.
60. Vincent Bates, "Music Education, Neoliberal Social Reproduction, and Play," *Action, Criticism, and Theory for Music Education* 20, no. 3 (2021): 92–93.
61. Bates, "Music Education," 92–93.
62. Sean Robert Powell, *The Ideology of Competition in School Music* (New York: Oxford University Press, 2023), 111.
63. For further discussion of potential relationships between play and competition, see chapter 5.
64. J. Scott Goble, "Neoliberalism and Music Education: An Introduction," *Action, Criticism, and Theory for Music Education* 20, no. 3 (2021): 9, https://doi.org/10.22176/act20.3.1.
65. Woodford, *Music Education.*
66. Woodford, *Music Education*, 72. See also Randall Allsup, "The Eclipse of Higher Education or Problems Preparing Artists in a Mercantile World," *Music Education Research* 17, no. 3 (2015): 251–61.
67. Michel Foucault, *The Birth of Biopolitics*, ed. Michel Senellart, trans. Graham Burchell (New York: Palgrave Macmillan, 2008), 239.
68. Angela McRobbie, *Feminism and the Politics of Resilience: Essays on Gender, Media and the End of Welfare* (Cambridge: Polity, 2020), 36.
69. McRobbie, *Feminism and the Politics of Resilience*, 36.
70. Taylor, *Music and Capitalism*, 4.
71. Andrew Marantz, "The Left Turn," *New Yorker*, May 31, 2021, 38.
72. Cathy Benedict, "Processes of Alienation: Marx, Orff and Kodaly," *British Journal of Music Education* 26, no. 2 (2009): 213–24.
73. Benedict, "Processes of Alienation," 217.

74. Benedict, "Processes of Alienation," 219.

75. Joseph Abramo, "The Phantasmagoria of Competition in School Ensembles," *Philosophy of Music Education Review* 23, no. 2 (2017): 150–70.

76. Abramo, "Phantasmagoria of Competition in School Ensembles."

77. Joseph Abramo, "Whence Culture and Epistemology? Dialectical Materialism and Music Education," *Philosophy of Music Education Review* 29, no. 2 (2021): 155–73.

78. Taylor, *Music and Capitalism*, 2.

79. Taylor, *Music and Capitalism*, 44.

80. Aróstegui, "Implications of Neoliberalism," 49.

81. Brown, *In the Ruins of Neoliberalism*, 23–53.

82. Brown, *In the Ruins of Neoliberalism*, 37.

83. Brown, *In the Ruins of Neoliberalism*, 13.

84. Michael Sandel, *The Tyranny of Merit: What's Become of the Common Good?* (New York: Farrer, Straus and Giroux, 2020), 194.

85. Verónica Gago, "Financialization of Popular Life and the Extractive Operations of Capital: A Perspective from Argentina," *South Atlantic Quarterly* 114, no. 1 (2015): 11–28.

86. Gago, "Financialization of Popular Life," 22.

87. Ritchey, *Composing Capital*, 120.

88. Krugman, *Arguing with Zombies*, 281.

89. Harvey, *Companion to Marx's Capital*, 173.

90. "Global Wealth Report 2021," *Credit Suisse*, June 2021, https://www.credit-suisse.com/about-us/en/reports-research/global-wealth-report.html.

91. Krugman, *Arguing with Zombies*, 259.

92. William Robinson, *The Rise of the Global Police State* (London: Pluto Press, 2020).

93. Robinson, *Rise of the Global Police State*, 77–78.

94. Zeus Leonardo, *Race Frameworks: A Multidimensional Theory of Racism and Education* (New York: Columbia University Press, 2013), 44–81.

95. Leonardo, *Race Frameworks*, 58–59.

96. Leonardo, *Race Frameworks*, 44–81.

97. Lead editor for the nonprofit organization Decolonizing the Music Room (https://www.decolonizingthemusicroom.com/) Lorelei Batislaong advocates using the terms Black, Brown, Indigenous, and Asian (BBIA) rather than Black, Indigenous, and People of Color (BIPOC). For additional discussion, see https://youtu.be/nMrlgoYmLUo.

98. Leonardo, *Race Frameworks*, 73.

99. Silvia Federici, *Beyond the Periphery of the Skin: Rethinking, Remaking, and Reclaiming the Body in Contemporary Capitalism* (Brooklyn: PM Press, 2020).

100. Federici, *Beyond the Periphery of the Skin*, 28.

101. McRobbie, *Feminism and the Politics of Resilience*, 76.
102. McRobbie, *Feminism and the Politics of Resilience*, 27.
103. Powell, *Ideology of Competition in School Music*, 43.
104. David A. Rickels, "Nonperformance Variables as Predictors of Marching Band Contest Results," *Bulletin of the Council for Research in Music Education* 194 (2012): 53–72.
105. Powell, *Ideology of Competition*, 50.
106. Powell, *Ideology of Competition*, 88.
107. Gareth Dylan Smith, "Neoliberalism and Symbolic Violence in Higher Music Education," in *Giving Voice to Democracy in Music Education*, ed. Lisa C. DeLorenzo (New York: Routledge, 2015), 76.
108. Cathy Benedict and Jared O'Leary, "Reconceptualizing 'Music Making': Music Technology and Freedom in the Age of Neoliberalism," *Action, Criticism, and Theory for Music Education* 18, no. 1 (2019): 26–43.
109. Joseph Abramo, "Whence Culture and Epistemology? Dialectical Materialism and Music Education," *Philosophy of Music Education Review* 29, no. 2 (2021): 168–69.
110. Harvey, *Companion to Marx's Capital*, 8.
111. Brown, *In the Ruins of Neoliberalism*; David Harvey, *Seventeen Contradictions and the End of Capitalism* (New York: Oxford University Press, 2014).
112. Harvey, *Companion to Marx's Capital*, 16.
113. Elizabeth Napolitano, "Warren Buffett Donates 870 Million to Charities before Thanksgiving," CBS News, November 22, 2023, https://www.cbsnews.com/news/warren-buffett-donates-870-million-to-charities-before-thanksgiving/.
114. Patel and Moore, *History of the World in Seven Cheap Things*, 199.
115. Krugman, *Arguing with Zombies*, 1–2.
116. Krugman, *Arguing with Zombies*, 313.
117. Peter Hudis, "Marx's Concept of Socialism," in *The Oxford Handbook of Karl Marx*, ed. Matt Vidal, Tony Smith, Tomás Rotta, and Paul Prew (New York: Oxford University Press, 2018), 767.
118. Alain Badiou, *The Communist Hypothesis*, trans. David Macey and Steve Corcoran (Brooklyn: Verso Books, 2010); Chantel Mouffe, *For a Left Populism* (Brooklyn: Verso Books, 2018); According to Harvey, Marx himself imagined communism as involving decentralized economies in which laborers control their own production process. Harvey, *Companion to Marx's Capital*, 440.
119. Harvey, *Companion to Marx's Capital*, 262.
120. Federici, *Patriarchy of the Wage*, 66.
121. Anna Bull, *Class, Control, and Classical Music* (New York: Oxford University Press, 2019).

122. Michel Foucault, *Power/Knowledge: Selected Interviews and Other Writings, 1972–1997,* ed. Colin Gordon, trans. Colin Gordon, Leo Marshall, John Mepham, and Kate Soper (New York: Pantheon Books, 1980).

123. See, for example, Telegraph, “Climate Activists Glue Themselves to a Conductor Stand at Beethoven Concert,” *YouTube,* accessed June 23, 2023, https://www.youtube.com/watch?v=qLlq9dLLwmU.

124. Federici, *Beyond the Periphery of the Skin.*

TWO

WILL POPULAR MUSIC SAVE US?

Limitations of Relevance and Flexibility

AT FIRST GLANCE, IT MIGHT appear that classical music-making practices reinforce contemporary capitalist ideals, while genres like hip-hop and rap challenge them. One need to look no further than the 2017 procapitalist opera *The (R)evolution of Steve Jobs* (recording available on Amazon) for an overt example of agreement between classical music and capitalist aims. By treating the production and evolution of the iPhone as a heroic act, the opera creators valorize ongoing consumption while hiding labor costs, with the exception of Job's own tormented relationships. More broadly, classical music is often consumed in halls built by the philanthropy of those in the wealthiest 1 percent (e.g., Carnegie Hall in New York City and the Walt Disney Concert Hall in Los Angeles), and arts leaders honor wealthy donors, including business magnates, with receptions and plaques.

Since classical music making also demands extensive training and expensive instruments often only available to members of the middle and upper classes, such practices entrench class inequalities prevalent within society at large.[1] After conducting a wide-ranging qualitative study of European conservatory musicians, Anna Bull concluded that "the middle classes' common commitment to education as a way to retain their social position suggests that classical music education is a particularly good way of both signaling and reproducing class position."[2] Additionally, the fierce, individualistic competition at elite classical music colleges and conservatories mirrors the competition, discipline, and individual responsibility central to capitalism.

However, other qualities of contemporary professional classical music making resist capitalist logic. As Randall Allsup explains, "it is an irony that while Western classical art music structures and is structured by capitalism's violence, the music conservatory remains strangely indifferent to the market."[3] For example, music degree programs rely heavily on one-to-one private lesson instruction, which often costs institutions more money than they receive from associated tuition.

Classical music endeavors can reinforce cultural capital important for retaining class relations, but due to their long-standing unprofitability, they do not directly enrich their leaders. Alternatively, popular music-making practices by definition reach a large number of people, potentially facilitating substantial profits for capitalist producers. Following the large popular music education organization Music Will, I understand *popular music* as including the genres of "rock, pop, R&B, Latin, rap and country."[4]

Central to justifying the inclusion of popular music practices in primary and secondary music education is the idea of relevance. While music education philosophers and policymakers have convincingly problematized exclusive focus on music education practices students deem irrelevant, meaning not valuable to their current and future selves, the possible drawbacks of emphasizing relevance remain largely absent from music education scholarship. I begin this chapter by considering how centering relevant music making might reinforce values and practices that benefit the capitalist class.

CAPITALISM AND RELEVANCE

Since at least the time of the 1967 Tanglewood Declaration, American music educators have asserted the need for music teaching and learning beyond the Western classical music canon. One of eight points in the Tanglewood Declaration reads: "Music of all periods, styles, forms, and cultures belongs in the curriculum. The musical repertory should be expanded to involve music of our time in its rich variety, including currently popular teenage music and avant-garde music, American folk music, and the music of other cultures."[5] Through the recent founding of the *Journal of Popular Music Education* and the American National Association for Music Education Popular Music Special Research Interest Group, the profession has made marked progress toward a more varied and relevant conception of American music education, and such aims have long been a part of K-12 music education in places like Scandinavia and New Zealand. Although many preservice teacher education programs in North and South America, Asia, and elsewhere still treat practices derived from Western art music making as primary, few contemporary music educators promote excluding popular music, folk music, and other musical practices from curricula.

Yet the need for increased engagement with relevant musical practices remains a central concern for music education leaders. In 2016, the College Music

Society Task Force for the Undergraduate Music Major (TFUMM) authored a document with recommendations based on the three pillars of creativity, diversity, and integration. Key to these recommendations is the importance of making music education relevant for contemporary society. For example, members of the TFUMM understand the theme of "content and delivery of a *relevant* yet rigorous curriculum that prepares students for musical engagement and leadership in an age of unprecedented excitement and avenues for growth [emphasis added]" as central to overhauling undergraduate music curricula.[6]

While these and other authors do not necessarily clarify how they define *relevant,* I take the word to mean "of contemporary interest."[7] This interest can include individuals' preferences; a student can find classical music making relevant even if their peers do not. However, in group music teaching and learning settings, relevance often refers to that which interests the largest number of students. Although interest can vary across geographic locations, popular music making is by definition relevant to many students. I offer that emphasis on relevance in music education corresponds with three central, interrelated processes that benefit capitalist producers: centering youth culture, furthering cultural omnivorousness, and holding attention.

YOUTH CULTURE: SELLING HIP (HOP)

Capitalism relies on the ongoing consumption of commodities. As detailed in chapter 1, when consumers purchase commodities, they pay more money than producers outlay in raw materials and labor wages, thus creating a profit for the capitalist class. The more commodities consumers purchase, the more the capitalist class benefits. Most forms of music making rely on commodities, ranging from music recordings to instruments to composition software. When music educators and students purchase such commodities, they benefit capitalist producers.

An ever-changing array of commodities spurs consumption. Since adults' cultural preferences tend to solidify over time,[8] capitalist market practices often rely on youth preferences, which change more quickly. In Timothy Taylor's words: "Children and adolescents aren't only targets—they are sources, the sources of the hip, the cool, the edgy. Their tastes, practices, and consumption habits are relentlessly and ruthlessly studied and marketed back to them. And everyone else."[9]

Music educators often understand relevance in terms of youth culture. For example, the Modern Band curriculum "teaches kids to perform, improvise and compose using the popular styles that they know and love including rock, pop, reggae, hip-hop, R&B and other modern styles."[10] Emphasizing music that students "know and love" while omitting attention to adult or community music making mirrors the role of youth culture within profit-driven music industries.

When music educators promote engagement with youth culture, they help create and sustain a market for new music commodities. Through such action, music educators facilitate what Karl Marx calls *rational consumption*.[11] According to Marx scholar David Harvey, rational consumption involves two conditions: members of the working class must have money available to purchase commodities and "have acquired consumption habits congenial to the absorption of the surplus product that capitalism perpetually generates."[12] Music making that students and teachers deem relevant, including popular music making, typically meets both of these conditions, as explained below.

First, while some families can and do spend huge sums of money on expensive musical instruments, show choir costumes, and elaborate marching band props, many middle- and lower-class parents cannot afford such luxuries. Furthermore, since local property taxes make up a significant portion of American K-12 schools' budgets, typically only schools in high property tax areas, in which many parents can already afford significant cultural expenditures, have the money to make such commodities widely available to students. Yet most parents can afford cheaper instruments like ukuleles, recordings of popular songs, and music streaming services. Focusing on relevant music making that relies on such purchases, in addition to ensembles such as band, choir, and orchestra, maximizes opportunities for spending on whatever music commodities parents, schools, and arts organizations can afford.

Second, since the music practices students deem relevant typically change from year to year, focusing on relevant music practices develops the dispositions needed for continual commodity consumption. Music educators engaging in relevant music practices must purchase necessary new music products, be they recordings, DJ software, or other commodities, while encouraging students to do the same. Such action plays a role in absorbing the aforementioned "surplus product that capitalism perpetually generates."[13] The fleeting nature of popular music practices, therefore, aligns more with the capitalist aim of ongoing consumption than the purchase of long-lasting resources, like musical instruments educators may use for decades.

CULTURAL OMNIVOROUSNESS

In addition to emphasizing youth culture, remaining musically relevant often involves a cultural omnivorousness.[14] For example, the TFUMM urges that in undergraduate music degree curricula, "engagement occur within a cultural expanse that is as broad as possible."[15] These authors clarify that rather than viewing diverse music making with "distanced fascination," undergraduates should develop improviser-composer-performer identities, assimilating and synthesizing "diverse influences that nurture intimate connections . . . with the rich diversity of the musical world."[16] Centering multiple music styles encourages more purchasing than narrow-focused emphasis on any one music genre.

In the aforementioned statement about Modern Band, a broad list of genres, ranging from reggae to hip-hop, is subsumed under the term *popular styles*.[17] While music educators may not teach all these practices, the statement implies that students should be familiar with them and that teachers should as well. In such instances, remaining musically relevant necessitates investing time and money to accumulate skills and resources associated with numerous, changing music styles. Although most educators continue developing their craft over the course of their careers, there exists a difference between deepening and expanding long-standing skill sets and aiming for relevance. The former generally emphasizes attention to qualitative differences, while the latter emphasizes quantities and accumulation, thus reinforcing ongoing capitalist consumption.

In addition to financially benefiting capitalist producers, remaining relevant through cultural omnivorousness can enhance one's position in globalized capitalist societies. Analyzing surveys completed by "high status persons," Richard Peterson and Roger Kern found that knowledge about a wide variety of cultural forms signaled cosmopolitan worldliness and reinforced one's upper-class standing.[18] Similarly, Joseph Abramo asserts that knowledge of diverse music making now holds more cultural capital than familiarity with only Western classical music and that cultural omnivorousness furthers the ongoing consumption from which capitalist producers profit.[19]

The flip side of emphasizing ongoing acquisition of diverse musical knowledge is that the capitalist class benefits from products meant to critique its practices. Taylor explains that even when artists, including rock musicians, portray themselves as counterculture or anticapitalist, the record industry still profits from their work.[20] For example, capitalist producers, who are overwhelmingly white, have profited from commodities ranging from music to clothing to signage created to show support for the Black Lives Matter movement.

Taylor adds that by constantly taking what is considered edgy and adapting it into consumable products, the music industry survives and assimilates the critiques contained within music making.[21] Music associated with the Black Lives Matter movement might encourage the questioning of the racial disparities within both the music industry and contemporary capitalist societies at large. Yet when the industry adopts, celebrates, and markets such music, it not only financially benefits from potentially subversive sentiments but also largely avoids race-related critiques. Similarly, consumers often focus on signaling their moral standing by displaying purchased Black Lives Matter commodities rather than advocating for changed laws and institutionalized practices. Absent other considerations, focusing on musical relevance—even edgy relevance—furthers, or at minimum distracts individuals from, existing inequitable capitalist practices.

In short, when music educators attend to the range of music making that youth deem relevant, they promote the capitalist ideal of continual acquisition. Such action benefits the capitalist class while subsuming potentially edgy critiques. Yet today, many people consume music not through the purchasing of individual songs but through streaming apps and websites. Such practices exemplify another aspect of ongoing consumption: the commodification of consumer attention.

HOLDING ATTENTION

Contemporary capitalist producers increasingly make a profit through the selling of platforms that enable unlimited consumption. Producers of services like Apple Music and Spotify want consumers to listen insatiably so that they continue to pay for a subscription. However, the capitalist aim of increased consumption can also be achieved when producers give away certain products for free to encourage the purchase of other commodities. As the clichéd saying goes, if you're not paying for it, you're the product being sold. This typically means that in the process of listening to free music or composing with free software, consumers see advertisements. Even in the case of paid subscription services like Spotify, advertisers, rather than listeners and musicians, are the primary customer.[22]

Since cultural choices can be an indicator of purchasing habits, advertisers target potential consumers based on their music preferences. Sellers might make a reasonable guess that a consumer who listens to songs from multiple boy bands likely purchases makeup or that someone who prefers hit tunes from the 1990s has an interest in nostalgic video games and movies. Companies can also sell consumers' music habits and personal information to marketing companies that create targeted advertisements. For example, companies target ads for Godiva chocolate to consumers listening to multiple songs about heartbreak.[23] The more music making can capture an individual's attention, the more potential profit is at stake. As such, both paid and free music platforms seek to hold consumers' attention for as long as possible.

For both students and teachers, the phrase "I find this music relevant" is often synonymous with the statement "This music captures my attention." Certainly, relevant music making can also provide participants comfort, insights about gender identity, or other understandings. Yet by definition, relevance first and foremost involves sustaining one's interest. Relevant music making need not facilitate meaningful self-knowledge and personal growth, and teachers seeking out such aims might prioritize them directly rather than focusing on relevance.

Music educators focused on relevant music making directly use the rhetoric of captured attention. For instance, a recent version of the Music Will website advertised that the group "pioneered a method of musical instruction that captures students' attention and imagination right away."[24] Such statements correspond with capitalist producers' emphasis on acquiring and holding consumers' attention.

In seeking to continue capturing a consumer's attention, producers of digital music platforms often focus less on musical content with the broadest social reach and more on individually tailored, continual sequences of music content. *New Yorker* writer Jia Tolentino explains that the goal of TikTok—and, I would add, every social network and video and audio streaming platform—is persuading viewers not to leave, a feat accomplished largely through algorithms that predict an individual's interests based on past behavior.[25] For example, the algorithm offers consumers who select Billboard Top 40 songs different music from those who select hip-hop or Afro Cuban jazz, simultaneously probing for additional interests that could prolong listening. In some sense, the algorithm "knows more about what we like than we do."[26] Stated differently, the producers of platforms enabling engagement with music that young people deem relevant draw on past preferences to hold individual viewers' attention for as long as possible. In the process, they curate aspects of listeners' current and possible future identities.

When music educators emphasize gripping and retaining students' attention, they function much like a TikTok or YouTube algorithm, reinforcing that aspect of capitalist logic. While most educative endeavors necessitate taking students' attention into account, centering relevance necessitates understanding capturing students' attention as a primary aim rather than a means to other ends and values.

FLEXIBLE WORKERS AND ZANY TEACHERS

In addition to highlighting the limitations of irrelevant music practices, music education scholars have problematized music educators' limited conceptions of musical expertise. Allsup argues that music educators define musical expertise primarily in terms of replicating prior standardized music practices.[27] He proposes the need for an expanded vision of expertise that foregrounds musical experimentation and ongoing learning: "Public music education requires that teachers have the flexibility to thoughtfully interact within musical and social arenas that are new."[28] Similarly, in the "innovative" music teaching and learning program at Arizona State University, highlighted as a model at the 2013 Society for Music Teacher Education Symposium,[29] "flexible musicians" serves as one of "four core principles."[30]

Calls for more flexible music teaching mirror and reinforce the adaptability needed to maintain employment within contemporary capitalist societies. In order to meet changing production practices, including making new products that spur consumption, the economy demands that workers constantly learn new skills. Harvey summarizes: "Capitalism requires fluidity and adaptability of labor, an educated and well-rounded labor force, capable of doing multiple tasks and able to respond flexibly to changing conditions."[31] While most professions benefit from ongoing curiosity and a degree of adaptability, understanding flexible pedagogy and musicianship as grounding principles or goals corresponds with contemporary capitalist values. In cultural theorist Sianne Ngai's words, the ideal worker of postindustrial capitalism is a "perpetual temp, extra, or odd-jobber—itinerate and flexible."[32]

Additionally, capitalist leaders have found that keeping a workforce in precarious conditions can improve productivity. For example, the world's second largest employer, Amazon, stops providing guaranteed wage increases after three years and offers incentives for low-skilled employees to quit, including courses that train them to enter other fields.[33] The *New York Times* reports: "Amazon's founder didn't want hourly workers to stick around for long, viewing 'a large, disgruntled' work force as a threat."[34] Flexible workers not only adapt to technological changes and other innovations at their current jobs but also rebound and reinvent themselves in the face of repeated termination and reemployment in new fields.

Music educators who provide students a smattering of skills, knowledge, and proficiencies as opposed to deep knowledge in one or two musical practices assist them in developing the dispositions needed to be precarious workers in the arts sector and beyond. In Marianna Ritchey's words, such musicians become "a specialist with no specialty—the ideal flexible neoliberal subject."[35] Teachers who enact flexibility as they move across diverse, relevant music practices become the ideal capitalist worker and model such identities for their students.

Ngai argues that this modeling is itself a contemporary aesthetic category, which she terms *zany*.[36] Providing an example of the zany, Ngai describes an *I Love Lucy* episode titled "The Ballet," in which Lucy Ricardo's "unfeminine failure to bend gracefully results in her leg getting stuck in the bar, the sitcom's 'zany [and] talentless housewife' is comical because of her failure to be as 'flexible' as required by the roles she assumes in her pursuit of paid work—an unremitting succession that in turn seems to be a formal echo of the multiple roles already demanded by the informal or unpaid job of housewife and mother (which also entails being a cook, teacher, chauffeur, cleaner, and more)."[37] One could make a similar observation about a flexible music educator unprepared to teach an ever-evolving list of relevant music genres and practices. The teacher who already specializes in classical, jazz, and hip-hop music might appear comical as they struggle to teach reggae, K-pop, and country music.

Moreover, students' ever-changing and increasingly individualistic music interests make it difficult for any music educator to keep pace. As Ritchey notes, few of even the most privileged musicians can stay skilled in the vast array of changing global music practices.[38] In summary, teachers might possess deep knowledge and skills in a few music areas, but when they strive for a musical flexibility they cannot realistically achieve, they may come across as zany and incompetent.

LIMITATIONS

Taken together, centering relevance and flexible musicianship has marked limitations. Such action promotes individualism while undermining collaboration, emphasizes issues of recognition over distribution, and equates capitalist market practices with ethical action. I address each of these three issues in turn.

First, focusing on relevance and flexibility often centers individuals', rather than diverse groups', preferences and concerns. While individual students should consider their own aims, such action becomes problematic when students focus on personal preferences without regard for others' needs or desires. Alasdair MacIntyre explains that members of capitalist societies tend to equate rational action with maximizing the satisfaction of their own preference.[39] Through such thinking, success becomes synonymous with fulfilling an individual's desires, while others' needs and preferences go unconsidered.[40]

Likewise, music educators centering relevant music making often valorize the process of students expressing a preference. Although some relevance-focused music educators, including proponents of culturally relevant pedagogy, call for the interrogation of problematic themes—such as violence or sexism—within youth-selected music,[41] even these educators rarely question the individual-centered preference process that underlies such selections. When music educators centering relevance take youth preferences as given, they enable the fulfillment of one's own desires to take precedence over the consideration of others' preferences, needs, and desires.

Focusing on individual musical preferences can also undermine group cohesion and cooperation. As Paul Louth explains: "Instant access to a theoretically unlimited supply of music easily untethered from its socio-cultural or historical origins, using highly individualized technology, has the potential to accelerate the flattening out of collective meanings associated with particular musical styles, gestures, or phrases."[42] When music educators foreground individual preference, they minimize opportunities for developing collective musical identities and communal cultural experiences. Such action can undercut group problem solving and shared responsibility. Although individuals, particularly those whose experiences and perspectives contrast dominant norms, ultimately need to share their unique perspectives during collaborative endeavors, such action differs from expressing personal likes and dislikes.

Challenging the pernicious aspects of contemporary capitalist practices necessitates a sense of communal responsibility and the skills to work alongside different individuals. Yet when relevance-focused music educators position majority opinion as the primary unit of concern, they de-emphasize the interests and concerns of students with minoritarian identities. While music educators should not continue long-standing practices that subsume divergent student identities under white middle-class norms, the limits of individualism, self-centeredness, and majority preference that often accompany the valuing of musical relevance necessitate further attention.

A second concern is that emphasizing relevance and flexible musicianship centers what philosopher Nancy Fraser explains as issues related to recognition, meaning awareness and attention to certain identities and interests, rather than distribution, meaning how wealth, resources, and power are allocated.[43] She contends that American Democrats aim for recognition of "diversity, multiculturalism, and women's rights," and American Republicans favor an ethnonational, anti-immigration, pro-Christian platform. Yet both parties support problematic stances on distribution-related issues, including free trade, low taxes, and a curtailing of labor rights.[44] Fraser argues that by keeping both sides locked in a debate over diversity versus nationalism, politicians avoid crucial populist agreement about the exploitation inherent in contemporary economic practices.

Likewise, calls for more relevant and flexible forms of music engagement center issues of recognition. In this logic, the teacher who emphasizes diverse music practices is superior to the one narrowly focused on one genre or skill set. While issues related to whose music and musical practices teachers and students recognize certainly deserve attention apart from considerations about the distribution of resources—within and across music programs and within societies at large—neither teacher is fundamentally challenging the material inequities key to capitalism. As Zeus Leonardo explains, when Black artists and artistic practices serve as entertainment, they divert attention from various forms of capitalist exploitation.[45] Furthermore, teachers focused on recognizing diverse music making typically reinforce the ongoing acquisition and consumption on which ever-expanding capitalism rests.

A third problem of the alignment between relevance, flexibility, and capitalism is that the free market can become a substitute for ethics. In contemporary capitalist societies, the perpetual satisfaction of one's personal desires often becomes synonymous with not only rational action but also ethical action.[46] Making a similar argument about trends in musicology, Ritchey explains: "In their efforts to deflate the pretentious universalizing of the canon's defenders, who insisted that authentic art constitutes a transcendent sphere, some musicologists have worked to center the market unproblematically as the only meaningful structuring principle for human life."[47] As such, what consumers deem relevant or important becomes a stand-in for the ethically good.

Assuming the ethical nature of relevance becomes particularly problematic when relevance relies on the unbounded consumption encouraged by contemporary capitalist profit-seeking practices. As MacIntyre observes, many people now treat the trait of acquisitiveness, which philosophers such as Aristotle and Aquinas understood as a vice, as a virtue and duty.[48] Similarly, writing about cultural practices, Pierre Bourdieu explains that the "new tastemakers" offer a "morality" based on the art of continual consumption.[49] Music educators who continually accumulate musical knowledge and skills in order to remain relevant may come to understand acquisition—of music recordings, skills, or knowledge—as its own end. As such, they may develop and promote an acquisition-oriented morality that treats unrestrained consumption as ethically good.

In noting potential limits of valuing relevance and flexible musicianship, I do not mean to suggest that these qualities are useless or unimportant. Any attempt to resist, challenge, or even just survive problematic aspects of contemporary globalized capitalism will likely involve relevant music making and flexible musicianship. However, when music educators understand musical relevance or pedagogical flexibility apart from other aims and values, they reinforce key capitalist values and dispositions. Moreover, when music educators understand relevance and flexibility as being good in an ethical sense, they minimize and undercut opportunities for profession-wide debates about what ethical music education should and might be.[50]

WILL POPULAR MUSIC SAVE US?

In addition to aiming for relevance and flexibility, music educators value certain types of music making over others. I began this chapter by showing how classical music practices, largely because of their ongoing association with bourgeois values, often reinforce the individualism and class hierarchies key to capitalism; however, certain classical music making may subvert or challenge capitalist ideals. For example, Emmanuel Chabrier pokes fun at wealth and royalty through his character King Ouf in the opera *L'Étoile,* and Giacomo Puccini illuminates the material struggles of lower socioeconomic class individuals in *La Bohème*. More recently, classical music making like Ted Hearne's composition *Privilege,* which includes texts questioning the nature of privilege and the treatment of individuals "unnecessary for the American economy,"[51] encourages awareness about the troubling systemic inequities embedded in capitalist systems.

Alternatively, hip-hop has traditionally been associated with antiestablishment content. Yet the hip-hop most individuals encounter by definition appeals to a broad range of people. Considering how popularity plays out in terms of race, Leonardo explains: "Mainstream Black artists' success is bound up with Whites' expectations of an acceptable Blackness. It is then no surprise that the narrowed choices for Black representation in musical lyrics, magazines, and other populist venues for *commercial hip hop* is tethered by White desires to either transform Blackness into palatable forms, such as Snoop Dogg's reality television show or Ice Cube's partnership with Martha Stewart, or criminalize it, as in the 1990s gangsta rap. The range in between, from the Black Eyed Peas to Nicki Minaj, becomes enjoyable spectacles that distract consumers from the workings of the political economy."[52] In other words, hip-hop musicians often either make anticapitalist messages more palatable for mainstream listeners or display them as an aspect of deviant culture to be enjoyed absent critical reflection.

Moreover, many hip-hop artists flaunt money and unrestrained consumption. For example, Cardi B's "Up" promotes a lifestyle of jewelry, Bentley cars, and Birkin bags (handbags costing $5,000–$10,000 USD). And while a handful of Black producers have economically benefited from hip-hop's success, the music industry executives who profit the most from mainstream hip-hop music are predominantly white.[53]

A similar narrative holds true for music genres like pop, rock, and country. Songs in these genres typically either ignore or reinforce capitalist ideals. Lyrics about heartbreak or romantic desire avoid references to economic practices or social ills, and Billboard's top song of the 2010s, Bruno Mars' "Uptown Funk," glamorizes expensive products like white gold and the St. Laurent brand. Popular songs like Lorde's "Royals," which advocates not caring about products like Cadillac cars and jet planes, have the potential to challenge capitalist desires. However, students replicating "Royals" or other anticapitalist songs may still leave such endeavors wishing to purchase more music or other commodities.

Unlike professional classical musicians, popular musicians do not typically need extensive elite training; they may therefore encounter fewer socioeconomic barriers to entering artistic spheres. As detailed in chapter 4, such music making can provide opportunities for lower- and middle-class students to improve their financial standing. Yet like individuals working in most artistic media, few popular artists become famous enough to profit significantly from their musical endeavors.

In short, neither the content nor the socioeconomic practices associated with classical or popular music, including hip-hop, necessarily challenge capitalist ideals. As such, music genre cannot serve as a sufficient indicator of the extent to which practices align with or provide alternatives to problematic aspects of contemporary capitalism.

Interestingly, one of the earliest and most prominent music writers to critique capitalism, Theodore Adorno, deemed certain music genres, particularly the atonal music composed by his intellectual contemporaries, as best suited to encourage an awakening about one's socioeconomic conditions.[54] While I find Adorno's centering of atonal music and dismissal of jazz and popular music indefensible, he makes an intriguing observation about the potential for certain music experiences to reflect one's own capitalist alienation back to them. For Adorno, this awareness occurs when music experiences interrupt individuals' passive acceptance of their place in capitalist societies.[55]

What if, rather than limiting this interruptive potential to certain music genres, teachers and students focused on the individual and collective sensations that constitute a specific musical experience? Although Adorno wrote well before the creation of what is now called affect theory, which focuses on the sensations that flow among people, his work in part aligns with such conceptualizations. Since affect theory offers a way to understand artistic experiences in terms of sensational flows, it avoids the limits of focusing on specific music genres or practices. In the following chapter, I explain affect theory and posit how it might provide insights about relationships between artistic events and capitalism. I also consider which ethical values might work against key problematic aspects of contemporary globalized capitalism.

NOTES

1. Anna Bull, *Class, Control, and Classical Music* (New York: Oxford University Press, 2019), 69.
2. Bull, *Class, Control, and Classical Music*, 6.
3. Randall Allsup, "The Eclipse of Higher Education or Problems Preparing Artists in a Mercantile World," *Music Education Research* 17, no. 3 (2015): 254.
4. Music Will, "About Music Will," *Music Will*, accessed June 23, 2023, https://musicwill.org/about/.
5. Allen Britton, Arnold Broido, and Charles Gary, "The Tanglewood Declaration," in *Documentary Report of the Tanglewood Symposium*, ed. Robert A. Choate (Washington, DC: Music Educators National Conference, 1968), 1.
6. Patricia Shehan Campbell, David Myers, and Ed Sarath, "Transforming Music Study from Its Foundations: A Manifesto for Progressive Change in the Undergraduate Preparation of Music Majors," *College Music Society*, 2016, https://www.music.org/pdf/pubs/tfumm/TFUMM.pdf, 1.
7. A quick Google search confirms this common definition of the term.
8. Thoy Ong, "Our Musical Preferences Peak as Teens, Says Study," *The Verge*, February 12, 2018, https://www.theverge.com/2018/2/12/17003076/spotify-data-shows-songs-teens-adult-taste-music.
9. Timothy Taylor, *Music and Capitalism: A History of the Present* (Chicago: University of Chicago Press, 2016), 65.
10. "Modern Band," *Little Kids Rock*, accessed July 8, 2021, https://www.littlekidsrock.org/the-program/modernband/.
11. Karl Marx, *Capital Volume II*, trans. David Fernach (New York: Penguin Books, 1993), 592.
12. David Harvey, *A Companion to Marx's Capital: The Complete Edition* (Brooklyn: Verso Books, 2018), 285.
13. Harvey, *Companion to Marx's Capital*, 285.
14. I take the term *cultural omnivorousness* from Richard Peterson and Roger Kerns, "Changing Highbrow Taste: From Snob to Omnivore," *American Sociological Review* 61, no. 5 (1996): 900–907.
15. Campbell, Myers, and Sarath, "Transforming Music," 5.
16. Campbell, Myers, and Sarath, "Transforming Music," 6.
17. "Modern Band."
18. Peterson and Kerns, "Changing Highbrow Taste."
19. Joseph Abramo, "What Does Culture Have to Do with Social Justice?" presentation, Society for Music Teacher Education Symposium, virtual, September 25, 2021.

20. Taylor, *Music and Capitalism*, 41.
21. Taylor, *Music and Capitalism*, 63.
22. Jack Morse, "How to Stop Spotify from Sharing Your Data, and Why You Should," *Mashable*, April 5, 2022, https://mashable.com/article/spotify-user-privacy-settings.
23. Morse, "How to Stop Spotify from Sharing Your Data."
24. "Frequently Asked Questions," *Little Kids Rock*, accessed July 8, 2021, https://www.littlekidsrock.org/about/faq/. In midst of working on this manuscript, the organization Little Kids Rock changed its name to Music Will and updated many of its webpages. The information cited here has been removed from the revised website.
25. Jia Tolentino, "How TikTok Holds Our Attention," *New Yorker*, September 30, 2019, https://www.newyorker.com/magazine/2019/09/30/how-tiktok-holds-our-attention.
26. Tolentino, "How TikTok Holds Our Attention."
27. Randall Allsup, *Remixing the Classroom* (Bloomington: Indiana University Press, 2016).
28. Allsup, *Remixing the Classroom*, 14.
29. Sandra Stauffer, Jill Sullivan, Margaret Schmidt, and Evan Tobias, "Aligning Conceptions and Capacity: Turning Visions into Reality," presentation, *Society for Music Teacher Education*, Greensboro, North Carolina, September 2013.
30. "A Degree in Music Teaching and Learning," *Arizona State University*, accessed July 8, 2021, https://musicdancetheatre.asu.edu/degree-programs/music/music-learning-and-teaching.
31. Harvey, *Companion to Marx's Capital*, 233.
32. Sianne Ngai, *Our Aesthetic Categories* (Cambridge, MA: Harvard University Press, 2012), 10.
33. "Inside Amazon's Employment Machine," *New York Times*, June 15, 2021, https://www.nytimes.com/interactive/2021/06/15/us/amazon-workers.html.
34. "Inside Amazon's Employment Machine."
35. Marianna Ritchey, *Composing Capital: Classical Music in the Neoliberal Era* (Chicago: University of Chicago Press, 2019), 70.
36. Ngai, *Our Aesthetic Categories*.
37. Ngai, *Our Aesthetic Categories*, 179.
38. Ritchey, *Composing Capital*, 70.
39. Alasdair MacIntyre, *Ethics in the Conflicts of Modernity: An Essay on Desire, Practical Reasoning, and Narrative* (Cambridge: Cambridge University Press, 2016), 102.
40. MacIntyre, *Ethics in the Conflicts of Modernity*, 135.
41. See, for example, Kate R. Fitzpatrick, "Cultural Diversity and the Formation of Identity: Our Role as Music Teachers," *Music Educators Journal* 98, no. 4 (2012): 58.

42. J. Paul Louth, “Music Education and the Shrinking Public Space,” presentation, International Symposium on the Sociology of Music Education, virtual, June 21, 2021.

43. Nancy Fraser, *The Old Is Dying and the New Cannot Be Reborn* (Brooklyn: Verso Books, 2019).

44. Fraser, *Old Is Dying and the New Cannot Be Reborn*, 15.

45. Zeus Leonardo, *Race Frameworks: A Multidimensional Theory of Racism and Education* (New York: Columbia University Press, 2013), 53.

46. MacIntyre, *Ethics in the Conflicts of Modernity*, 102.

47. Ritchey, *Composing Capital*, 12.

48. MacIntyre, *Ethics in the Conflicts of Modernity*, 109.

49. Pierre Bourdieu, *Distinction: A Social Critique of the Judgement of Taste*, trans. Richard Nice (Cambridge, MA: Harvard University Press, 1984), 311.

50. Wayne Bowman has long advocated for such debates. See, for example, Wayne Bowman, “Music as Ethical Encounter (Charles Leonhard Lecture, University of Illinois),” *Bulletin of the Council for Research in Music Education* 151 (2001): 11–20.

51. Ted Hearne, “Privilege,” accessed June 23, 2023, https://www.tedhearne.com/works/privilege.

52. Leonardo, *Race Frameworks*, 53.

53. Stacy L. Smith, Carmen Lee, Marc Choueiti, Katherine Pieper, Zoe Moore, Dana Dinh, and Artur Tofan, “Inclusion in the Music Business: Gender & Race/Ethnicity Across Executives, Artists & Talent Teams,” *USC Annenberg*, June 2021, https://assets.uscannenberg.org/docs/aii-inclusion-music-industry-2021-06-14.pdf.

54. Theodor Adorno, *Aesthetic Theory*, trans. Robert Hullot-Kentor (Minneapolis: University of Minnesota Press, 1997), 2.

55. Adorno, *Aesthetic Theory*, 22.

THREE

AFFECTIVE FLOWS AND ETHICAL COMMITMENTS

IMAGINE THREE CLASSROOMS LISTENING TO the same recording of Seattle hip-hop group Blue Scholars' song "Proletariat Blues," which addresses how capitalist producers exploit working-class persons. In one classroom, the students sit silently in separate rows; following their teacher's instructions, they listen intently to the percussion line with the aim of describing it. In the second space, the teacher encourages students to tap along with the percussion line, and the students giggle as they try to keep pace and add their own improvisations. In the third classroom, students have the option of writing words that come to mind as they hear the artists' tales of injustice or drawing a picture about how the song makes them feel. While all the teachers and students might agree that the song's upbeat tempo and mournful lyrics communicate muted anger, participants' individual and collective emotional experiences likely differ across the three locations. Although listeners might agree on what emotion the song's creators aimed to induce, teachers' and students' immediate circumstances—including intersections among individuals' sensational experiences or lack thereof—inform how they make meaning out of the lesson.

Beginning in the 1970s, emotion served as a key component of Bennett Reimer's philosophy. While emphasizing the ineffability of individuals' affective responses to music, Reimer drew on Susanne Langer's work to consider the role of emotional communication in music education.[1] David Elliott, writing alone and with Marissa Silverman, critiqued and added nuance to Reimer's ideas, providing increased attention to social context but maintaining the centering of emotion as a key aspect of music education.[2]

Focusing on emotion alone does not fully account for the different atmospheres in the aforementioned classrooms. Students in all three scenarios may experience happiness, anger, or frustration, but the extent to which emotions collectively intensify, evolve, or dissipate likely varies significantly. A deeper understanding of these variations necessitates attending not just to emotions or sensations but to their movement, including how they flow between and among individuals during artistic endeavors. Stated differently, since similar social contexts may incite markedly different sensational flows, the nature and directionality of flows necessitates attention.

In addition to creating contrasting emotional atmospheres, the speed and directionality of sensational flows can mirror certain capitalism-related flows. As detailed in chapter 1, capitalism relies on the circulation of values. Specific contexts determine the use and exchange values of commodities, and these values change over time. In order to increase profits, capitalist producers aim for ever-increasing exchange values.

Artistic sensations that both accelerate and flow outward, perhaps enraging more and more individuals, parallel continually expanding capitalist growth. As detailed in chapter 4, such sensations can directly promote capitalist accumulation. And even when expanding artistic sensations do not immediately contribute to profit creation for capitalist producers, they often promote the self-centeredness on which capitalism thrives. Alternatively, sensations that turn inward and dissipate contrast capitalist growth trajectories.

If music educators and students aim to understand how their practices might correspond with or contradict key aspects of capitalism, then considering sensational flows, as opposed to individuals' feelings, takes on added importance. Yet expanding sensational flows that parallel capitalist growth may still address capitalist ills. For example, continually increasing anger aimed at confronting the problematic nature of material inequities could lead to policy changes that reduce capitalist imbalances. As such, it is necessary to consider both the trajectories of sensational flows and their content, including their potential to support ethical commitments that address capitalist ills.

The purpose of this chapter is twofold. First, I consider why focusing on sensational flows, also known as affective flows, rather than on categories of musical practices or genres might have increased potential to illuminate and inform relationships between music education and capitalism. Second, I propose two ethical commitments that may address key problematic aspects of contemporary globalized capitalism.

AFFECTIVE FLOWS: AN INTRODUCTION TO AFFECT

Although authors utilizing affect theory purposely resist providing a single, generalizable definition of it,[3] understanding *affect* as synonymous with *intensity* may serve as an initial explanation. In a prominently cited 1995 essay entitled "The Autonomy of Affect," Brian Massumi distinguishes between the quality and intensity of an image.[4] Viewers typically experience the quality of an image with reference to intersubjective artistic contexts.[5] The detailing on a vase may exemplify the highest quality Ming Dynasty designs, for example. Similarly, one might evaluate a swing-era jazz trumpet improvisation as high quality because it evokes what they imagine as a perfect improvisation within that style of music. These qualitative judgments are narrative in that they involve expectation and continuity.[6] Viewers expect certain colors and shapes on a Ming vase and certain notes and phrasings in a swing-era jazz trumpet solo, and these expectations contribute to how audiences evaluate quality.

Intensity, however, involves "automatic reactions most directly manifested in the skin."[7] A hastily painted bright red canvas may lack quality, indicate no narrative, and fail to meet preset viewer expectations, yet its mere presence in a room of meticulously painted canvases may evoke more intensity than the surrounding images. Viewing the red canvas may cause one's heart rate to quicken, skin to tighten, and arm hairs to stand on end. This description is first and foremost intensive and thus affective.

Intensities—or affects—become feelings when individuals insert them into language and symbol systems, making them static and narrative in the process.[8] In Massumi's words, feeling "is qualified intensity."[9] Experiencing the red canvas, an individual might draw on previous associations with red images, such as warning signs, and experience anger. Alternatively, they might think about how a certain phrase in the jazz improvisation reminds them of a song they heard at a grandparent's funeral. Narrativizing the phrase as relating to that event, they might feel saddened. In each case, the experience of affective intensity coheres through symbolic and language associations, which qualify it as a specific feeling.[10]

An individual's recognition of their feelings suspends rather than stops these intensities.[11] Intense affects continue flowing throughout space regardless of whether individuals recognize them as feelings. Sianne Ngai explains first- versus third-person speech as distinguishing feelings from affects.[12] Feeling is contained by an identity—a speaking I—while affect belongs to the analysist's space, moving among identities.[13] I might experience the feeling of sadness during the performance of a mournful song, but someone viewing the entire performance space may observe how sad affects move among event participants over time. While feelings reside within sentient beings, affects vibrate freely throughout space.

Stated differently, affects are "forces of encounter" that connect individuals while also overflowing beyond them.[14] For example, imagine affects emerging from the aforementioned red canvas. If an individual viewer experiences these intensities as anger, then their body might tense and eyebrows tilt slightly downward. These physical changes produce further intensities that circulate among other nearby viewers.

Circulating affects integrate with other viewers' intensive, feelingful experiences of the painting. Since one person's expression of anger can influence another's reaction, humans who experience affects contribute to their amplification. However, because affects escape confinement within any one body, they retain a certain autonomy.[15] The flowing of affects creates connections among arts participants, but affects remain distinct entities rather than the property of any one participant.

Affects do not follow predictable trajectories. Angry intensities within a musical event could encourage various degrees of anger within participants, and this circulation would determine whether the angry affects grow or dissipate. Some participants may respond to angry affects with excitement or fear. Affects thus involve a "not yet" and potential "for extending further still."[16]

While individuals cannot necessarily guess how affective flows will propagate, they can observe changes in affective flows over time. For example, one may observe affective excitement at a rock concert vibrating more intensely among attendees and performers during the climax of a song. By examining both how affects have moved in the past and their temporary trajectories in the present, educators and students can describe affective flows at hand. However, since affects have a potentiality that can change course at any instant, their precise future motion resists comprehensive predictions. This unpredictability means that descriptions of affective flows are necessarily fleeting and incomplete.

In summary, affects are intense and vibratory. While they may temporarily cohere as feelings within individuals, they continue flowing among and beyond them. Given that affects continually fluctuate, individuals cannot necessarily predict their future trajectories.

AFFECTIVE FLOWS AND CAPITALISM

Although the trajectories of affective flows resist easy description, considering two qualities—intensity and vibratory pace—can serve as a starting point for examination. First, affective flows involve a certain intensity, ranging from minimal to extreme. A large crowd erupting at the end of a country music concert would likely involve extremely intense affective flows, while a parent singing a lullaby would typically involve intimate, minimally intense affective flows. These intensities can increase or decrease with each moment.

Second, the vibrations within an affective flow, like the tempo of a song, can have varying paces. They can move faster, remain constant, or slow as well as be continuous, hesitant, steady, or pausing and restarting. While the vibratory rate of intense affective flows often increases, this is not always the case. The affects of an intense musical climax can circulate quickly, or they can slowly linger, perhaps causing anxiety, joy, or anticipation.

Although affective flows have always emerged and propagated during artistic endeavors, the ever-increasing pervasiveness of virtual interactions, including on social media, has made them more prevalent and intense. *New Yorker* author Hua Hsu explains that affect theory can frame "uniquely modern questions," including, "Where did the seeming surplus of emotionality that we see on the Internet come from, and what might it become?"[17] Prior to the internet, affects emerging from one's musical accomplishments typically circulated among a limited group of family and friends. Yet at present, one can post a solo performance or new composition on social media, potentially creating far-reaching affective flows.

Additionally, Hsu notes that the motion-filled, unpredictable nature of affects, as opposed to more cohesive narratives, parallels the precarity of modern life.[18] One's entrepreneurial artistic practices can receive widespread praise on social media one day and little notice the next, thus defying a clear narrative. Attending to the evolving, unpredictable nature of affective flows rather than the feelings one expects a musical endeavor to arouse can assist students in better understanding the uncertain nature of feelingful experiences, including beyond the classroom.

More specifically, if capitalism is a process of value circulation,[19] then it is best compared to other circulating processes rather than to categories or other static distinctions. As such, focusing on how affective flows circulate during artistic endeavors may reveal more about parallels between music making and capitalism than focusing on genres of music or differences between musical practices. Yet correspondences between affective flows and capitalist flows, including degree of intensity and speed, do not necessarily mean that the former directly influences the latter, or vice versa. Since affective flows can both promote and undermine ethical aims, ethical positions that might enable music educators and students to combat key capitalist ills necessitate attention.

KEY CAPITALIST ILLS

Considering ethical commitments that can challenge pervasive problems in current capitalist societies demands examining the mechanisms underlying such ills. Contemporary globalized capitalism values profit above all else. As explained in chapters 1 and 2, this centering of profit creates and reinforces various arbitrary inequities, including ableism, classism, racism, and sexism. Given these disparities, individuals may choose to use their limited resources to address a single problematic issue. One may devote their life to securing environmental protections, greater access to college for immigrants, or more equal pay for women and LGBTQ+ individuals. While such work is desperately needed, it is also important to understand the root causes of these social hierarchies.

Pyramidal Exploitation

Capitalism is built on a pyramidal divide between the capitalist class, which owns the means of production, and the working class. The more the capitalist class exploits the working class, the more profit it makes, further solidifying its position at the top of the pyramid. Most humans, as well as all natural resources, end up on the lowest parts of the capitalist pyramid.

As long as the capitalist pyramid remains in place, workers will look for ways to better their position within it. This search inevitably leads to the creation of arbitrary hierarchies based on qualities such as race and ethnicity. Since addressing racial inequities absent attention to the pyramidal structures of capitalism often ends up pitting workers from different races—or with other contrasting characteristics—against each other, such action undermines opportunities for collective worker organization and provides the capitalist class further opportunities for worker exploitation. While capitalism does not account for all aspects of racism, sexism, and other inequities, I understand it as a primary contributor to these ills.

Rather than a pyramid, sociologist Arlie Hochschild, who spent five years immersed in a rural, very conservative Louisiana community, explains that community members understand their socioeconomic positionality through the imagery of a single file line. Interviewees perceived themselves as waiting patiently in a long line, hoping to reach the American dream.[20] For such individuals, "it's scary to look back; there are so many behind you, and in principle you wish them well. Still, you've waited a long time, worked hard, and the line is barely moving. You deserve to move forward a little faster."[21] While contemporary globalized capitalist practices are the primary cause of interviewees' financial woes, Hochschild explains that workers perceive immigrants and others "cutting" in the metaphorical line as the source of their stalled economic progress.[22]

The disproportionate racial and ethnic makeup of all rungs on the capitalist pyramid is highly problematic, but simply replacing one set of exploited workers (e.g., Black, Brown, or Indigenous) with another (e.g., white) does not fundamentally address the material inequities created by current enactments of capitalism. Absent significant government intervention, most members of capitalist economies will always exist on the lowest and thus most exploitable rungs of the pyramid. As such, the capitalist pyramidal structure and its resulting line imagery necessitate critique.

Moreover, when the workers Hochschild interviewed noted the slow pace of the line, they intuited another aspect of capitalist material inequity: the continual speeding up of capitalist exploitation. Hardworking laborers enable the capitalist class to accumulate more wealth, which it in turn uses to further exploit an even more economically desperate working class.[23] Absent government intervention or significant collective organizing, material inequities between producers and workers grow ever larger.

One might argue that education can enable students to move up the capitalist pyramid. In chapter 4, I explore how music education might contribute to such advancement. However, focusing on education as a remedy for capitalist ills is problematic for two reasons.

First, educational opportunities are far from equitable. For example, only one-third of students at Harvard and Stanford come from families earning incomes in the bottom 80 percent of American households, with only 4 percent of students coming from the bottom 20 percent. Likewise, more students from families in the top 1 percent of income earners attend Ivy League colleges than students from families in the bottom half of the United States income distribution combined.[24] Across P-12 public schools, there similarly exist staggering differences in per-pupil spending as well as huge disparities in access to music education and other opportunities. For instance, in Alabama the 2022 expenditure per pupil ranged from $9,176 to $19,436.[25]

Second, as exemplified by the inability of many college graduates to pay back student loans, more education does not fundamentally alter a system designed to benefit an elite few. The ever-increasing speed of capitalism means that, absent intervention, material differences between the capitalist class and everyone else will continue to widen. Educational qualifications increasingly enable one to compete for ever-scarcer middle-class jobs without any guarantee of attainment. In short, the exploitative structures key to contemporary capitalism are a primary ethical concern.

Alienation

In addition to material inequities, capitalist practices further a sense of individual and collective alienation. Karl Marx observes that because capitalist producers own the commodities over which workers labor, workers feel increasingly depleted.[26] For example, TikTok, a company valued at $50 billion in 2023, pays creators between $0.02 and $0.04 per thousand views.[27] When musicians neither reap the full monetary benefits of their labor nor feel empowered to alter their economic destinies, they often feel alienated from what they produce. In sociologist Harmut Rosa's words, "alienation thus indicates a state in which the world cannot be 'adaptively transformed' and so always appears cold, rigid, repulsive, and nonresponsive."[28]

Individuals living under contemporary globalized capitalist systems may also experience alienation beyond the workplace. As detailed in chapter 1, modern entrepreneurial individuals continue laboring outside of directly mandated working hours. On social media, individuals constantly brand themselves through posts, aiming to build far-reaching and robust social networks. This blurring of leisure and work time means that contemporary individuals may continually experience alienation.

Additionally, face-to-face communal engagements have become increasingly rare. Sociologist Robert D. Putnam meticulously documented that by the year 2000, the average American spent more time watching television and less time engaging in communal social groups, ranging from civic clubs to religious groups to bowling leagues, than they did in the 1950s and 1960s. More recently, engaging online has surpassed watching television as individuals' dominant leisure activity. The average global internet user ages sixteen to sixty-four spends nearly seven hours per day online and two hours and twenty-seven minutes on social media.[29] Despite these social interactions, individuals increasingly report feelings of loneliness. Economist Noreena Hertz summarizes that, as a result of contemporary capitalist practices, in the United States and United Kingdom, almost half of children and young adults report feeling lonely, and in Australia, Canada, the United States, and most of Europe, the percentage of fifteen-year-olds who report feeling lonely at school rose between 2003 and 2015.[30]

Moreover, while individuals can have important dialogue about the common good on social media platforms, customized, politically polarized newsfeeds paired with exaggerated or false information presented on various platforms means that Americans have less and less of a starting point for civil political conversations. Rather than deeming a policy or position problematic, individuals increasingly perceive political opponents as evil and unethical, further alienating themselves from fellow community members. As Rosa explains, alienation arises when "subject and world confront each other with indifference or hostility (repulsion) and thus without any inner connection."[31] When individuals demonize those with different political values, they undermine opportunities for meaningful social interactions that could provide a respite from alienation. The resulting lack of shared responsibility also undermines opportunities for collectively addressing capitalism-related problems. Absent worker collaboration, capitalist producers can worsen working conditions, which result in greater alienation.

In summary, life in contemporary capitalist societies involves increasing alienation through working conditions that alienate workers from the products of their labor and decreasing amounts of face-to-face communal activities. Politically polarized social media feeds and other information sources dissuade community members from the meaningful conversations and collective action needed to challenge capitalist exploitation. As such, music educators and students might benefit from added attention to the nature of capitalist exploitation and alienation.

OVERCOMING PROBLEMATIC ISSUES OF CONTEMPORARY GLOBALIZED CAPITALISM: LIMITS OF OPEN AND IDENTITY-FOCUSED ETHICS

Ethical decision-making involves not only having values but ordering those values. For instance, students and teachers might deem both self-discipline and equitable opportunities for achievement worthwhile values, but favoring the former over the latter fosters markedly different educational practices, and vice versa. Contemporary music education ethical philosophies tend to foreground two qualities that may inhibit the confronting of capitalist pyramidal structures.

First, music education philosophers (me included) often emphasize an open, process-oriented ethics. For example, Randall Allsup and Heidi Westerlund have proposed a situational ethics grounded in imagination and student-teacher dialogue, and more recently, Allsup has called for an ethics focused on possibilities and openness to what students can become.[32] Similarly, Patrick Schmidt asserts an ethics that acknowledges complexity and uncertainty within music teaching and learning, while I offer an ethics centering potentialities and perspective taking.[33] Philosophers focusing on the ideal of *Bildung*, a German concept that refers to personal development and self-cultivation through education and intellectual enrichment, likewise understand ethics as evolving in integration with educational journeys.[34] For all these authors, the qualities of ethical decision-making processes take precedence over claiming specific values to guide ethical judgments.

When music education philosophers focus on the qualities of ethical decision-making processes, like complexity and imagination, absent specific ethical aims, they allow those qualities to become their own ends. Yet values like complexity and imagination alone do little to address capitalist ills. A student open to possibilities can still engage in unquestioned commodity consumption or alienate themselves through isolated composing that profits TikTok investors.

Second, when music educators attend to specific ethical values, they often center what Nancy Fraser explains as issues of recognition rather than distribution.[35] For example, music educators have called for ending white supremacy, creating equity for students and teachers of all genders and sexual orientations, and foregrounding the voices of students with disabilities, all of which center the recognition of certain identities.[36] Calls for recognition have value; Fraser ultimately imagines "joining a robustly egalitarian politics of distribution to a substantively inclusive, class-sensitive politics of recognition."[37] However, centering recognition alone can only alter who resides on the bottom rungs of the capitalist pyramid, leaving the vast material inequities key to contemporary capitalism unchallenged.

Alternatively, distributive arguments "convey a view about how society should allocate divisible goods, especially income. This aspect speaks to the economic structure of society and, however obliquely, to its class divisions."[38] Attending to inequities in resource distribution questions the very nature of contemporary capitalist pyramidal structures and may encourage the imagining and demanding of alternative arrangements. Given the limits of both open, process-oriented ethics and value-focused ethics that center identity recognition, what might music educators and students aiming to counter capitalist exploitation and alienation consider?

I offer that addressing capitalist ills necessitates normative ethics. Education philosopher Quentin Wheeler-Bell argues that in addition to drawing on empirical evidence to demonstrate and critique forms of oppression and domination, critical research should involve normative theory. He explains normative theory as the philosophical articulation of "the principles and values that ought to govern society, as well as the principles that ought to govern the formal and informal educational arenas."[39] Taking a normative ethical stance necessitates selecting and defending specific social ends—as opposed to ambiguous processes—that teachers and students should prioritize. Given exploitative capitalist pyramidal structures and their resulting alienation, I propose two normative ethical commitments that music educators and students might consider: greater material equity and resonant engagements.

GREATER MATERIAL EQUITY

The exploitative pyramidal structures key to contemporary capitalist practices make aiming for greater material equity a primary concern. Committing to greater material equity involves asking how and why societies distribute material resources and acting to create more just distributions. While the distribution of symbols, such as Black Lives Matter images, may impact the distribution of resources, centering greater material equity avoids instances in which individuals display or use symbols absent sustained effort to change how they and others allocate finite resources, including money, materials, and time.

Importantly, I chose the term *equity* rather than *equality* because the completely equal distribution of resources is not necessarily equitable. For example, the equal distribution of educational resources may significantly disadvantage students with physical or cognitive disabilities. Given the vast material inequities within current capitalist societies, music educators and students can work toward greater material equity even absent a clearly defined end point. Which aspects of material equity music educators emphasize depends on how they understand their aims in relation to capitalism.

While I explore specific possibilities for addressing material inequities in the following four chapters, music educators might begin by evaluating the distribution of resources within their music programs and communities. These resources range from sheet music to instruments to computers and software. They may also include uniforms or costumes, private lessons, and field trips, including to competitions. Music educators centering material equity would provide added resources to students with the greatest material needs. If students with the greatest material needs remain absent from elective music education classes, then the nature of those courses should be reconsidered in order to center such students.

Educators' time, in the form of both class offerings and extracurricular activities, is also a resource that can directly impact material equity. Imagine a secondary music educator who teaches four periods per day of elective music ensembles that necessitate financial investment in the form of instruments, program fees, transportation beyond school hours, and other costs; the educator spends two periods per day teaching music classes open to all students, in which the school supplies all materials. By providing more course offerings that favor economically privileged students, the educator's time distribution reinforces existing societal material inequities. Centering material equity would redistribute this time so that most music classes were open to all students without added financial burdens or exclusionary commitments.

Centering material equity within required general music classes necessitates considering who enjoys and achieves within such spaces. If materials and activities appeal to students from financially well-off families, as often happens through the centering of Western art music and white popular music practices, then they do little to challenge existing societal inequities. Likewise, if assessments indicate that students from lower socioeconomic households achieve less than students from higher socioeconomic households, then class content, including assessments, necessitates revision. In arguing that music educators center material equity, I am not asserting that they should never assist financially well-off students who dedicate significant time and energy to their craft. Yet given that those students often have the resources to succeed absent significant teacher intervention, their achievements need not serve as a music program's primary focus.

Looking across programs, centering material equity also demands questioning how resources are distributed throughout a community or school district. Do the students in a wealthier section of town attend schools with greater access to the arts? What would it mean to make music education more widely available in communities with the lowest property values? What constitutes equitable distribution is always context specific, and any redistribution efforts should center the voices of those receiving the resources. In other words, music educators should not paternalistically decide what resources students and communities need absent input from those individuals. Although music educators alone will not fundamentally change the vastly unequal resource distribution within contemporary capitalist societies, their refusal to participate in furthering such practices could counter the pervasive reinforcement of inequitable capitalist ideals and inspire educators in other subjects, as well as communities at large, to do the same.

RESONANT ENGAGEMENTS

Overcoming the alienation pervasive in capitalist societies necessitates alternatives to competitive, self-centered ways of relating with one another and with nature. Rosa posits resonance as the antithesis of alienation.[40] According to Rosa, resonance involves a "responsive relation or 'vibrating wire' between subject and world" that is "cognitive, affective, and bodily."[41] As opposed to a mute relationship, in which the subject approaches the world—including other people—as stagnant and separate from themselves, resonant relationships involve a rippling back and forth between subject and surroundings.

Both transformation and nonassimilation play a key role in resonant relationships. Resonance involves "adaptive transformation" that mutually influences the subject and world.[42] Rosa elaborates: "Being *touched* or affected always means that one's relationship to the world becomes more fluid, with the result that self and world both emerge from the encounter changed."[43] This transformation necessitates subjects who feel capable to impact but not dominate or deplete other individuals and the natural world.[44] As such, altering the world through adaptive transformation differs from appropriating the world through the expansion of one's resources.[45]

Additionally, transformation necessitates resisting immediate confirmation or unconsidered agreement. The "Other" in a resonant relationship cannot merely be a copy of oneself.[46] Both entities must remain closed enough "so as to each speak in their own voice, while also remaining open enough to be affected or reached by each other."[47] For instance, since resonant relationships necessitate a willingness to contradict, a student who automatically defers to a teacher's interpretation of a musical line resists resonance.

More broadly, resonance involves individuals working together for the common good (associative) while maintaining the distinct voices needed for dissent (dissociative).[48] This meeting of agreement and contradiction results in the interdependence key to collaborative action.[49] Music makers who contribute to a music composition equally and uniquely, including through moments of tension and compromise, likely experience resonance with each other.

Rosa understands resonance as a way one can choose to relate with the world. Yet regardless of one's choice, Rosa asserts that the desire for resonance shapes human experience: "Human beings are existentially shaped by their longing for resonant relationships."[50] While this longing may inform individuals' decisions, Rosa argues that resonance can also serve as an ethical ideal. When adopted as an ethical aim, "resonance becomes a normative concept where it is established as a measure of the successful life."[51] Likewise, I understand resonance as an ethical ideal that may assist music educators and students in countering capitalist alienation.

While Rosa tends to talk about resonant relations, I instead focus on resonant engagements. Engagement implies a more sustained meeting than relation. Brief, precarious relations of any kind can still encourage alienation; the sustained aspect of longer-lasting resonant engagements has greater potential to overcome the alienation of modern capitalist life.

Given my critique of open ethics, one might ask whether centering resonant engagements shares similar limitations. Although understanding resonant engagement as an ethical demand enables a variety of actions, the aforementioned clarifications about resonance provide a more robust ethical framework than general calls for openness or complexity. Additionally, a certain amount of ethical openness avoids the problems of paternalism, in which teachers and students feel a significant lack of agency. Pairing the more open ethical commitment of resonant engagements with the more directed ethical aim of greater material equity provides a normative framework that is focused yet amenable to varying possibilities.

AFFECTIVE DISTRIBUTIVE RESONANCES

Thus far, I have treated the two purposes—the possibilities of affective flows in relation to capitalism and ethical commitments that confront key ills of contemporary globalized capitalism—separately. Yet focusing on affective flows, as opposed to music genres or types of musical practices, enhances awareness about how specific practices may support or inhibit ethical commitment to greater material equity. For example, a music educator centering affective flows would recognize that one group of students engaging in hip-hop music making may incite self-aggrandizing affective flows by attempting to out-do each other and promote their work on social media.

Alternatively, a second group of students engaging in the same genre (hip-hop) may invoke disruptive affective flows by aiming to expose racial wealth gaps and unsettling listeners' complacency. In this example, the affective flows, more so than the genre, reveal to what extent a music education endeavor can reinforce or challenge key aspects of capitalism. Although music educators should critically examine which genres and practices they teach, making affective flows a primary consideration may enable a clearer focus on the ethical aim of material equity.

Additionally, affect plays a key role in resonant engagements. In Rosa's words, resonance is "formed through affect and emotion."[52] Yet the presence of affect alone does not indicate resonance. Self-focused or exploitative affective experiences resist the self-world vibrations needed for resonant engagements. Attending to the nature of affective flows can therefore reveal whether a musical experience involves resonance.

In chapters 4 through 7, I consider how music educators and students might position themselves with respect to capitalism, including the possibilities of thriving within, surviving under, resisting, and challenging capitalist practices. In each chapter, I describe what affective flows might contribute to the positionality. Thriving within capitalism might involve fast, constantly expanding affective flows, while surviving under capitalism could involve playful, traceless affective flows. Resisting capitalism might involve dialogic affective flows that at times intensify toward shared ends. Inciting disruptive, response-inducing affective flows may contribute toward the challenging of capitalist ills.

It is important to clarify that these four broad categories of affective flows can overlap and integrate. A musical event that favors self-aggrandizing competition in one moment can turn playful in the next. Some participants may experience the event in ways that reinforce key capitalist values, while others might experience it in ways that resist or challenge capitalist inequities. As such, the following chapters provide a starting point for considering relationships between musical moments and capitalism rather than a solidified set of boundaries.

Alongside attention to affective flows, in chapters 4 through 7 I consider how ethical commitments to greater material equity and resonant engagements might play out in each of the four positionalities. Although aiming to thrive under capitalism necessarily reinforces capitalist ills, music educators and students might consider how commitment to greater material equity informs which students teachers support most during thriving-related processes. Alternatively, since resonance counters capitalist alienation, survival-focused music educators and students might center resonant engagements. While my conception of surviving capitalism does not directly challenge overarching injustices, music educators might emphasize resonant music making for students facing the greatest material inequities. Resisting capitalism involves highlighting how a commitment to resonant, communal engagements, particularly with people and places experiencing material inequities, could enable skills and dispositions needed for sustained cooperation with diverse others, including forms of civic engagement that can address capitalist ills. On the other hand, challenging capitalism directly focuses on music education practices that could facilitate greater material equity.

Rather than singular or sequential paths, I envision the four practices of thriving, surviving, resisting, and challenging like the opportunities in a *Choose Your Own Adventure* book.[53] In such books, readers return again and again to the start, selecting different paths each time. Likewise, music educators and students might, for example, choose to focus on surviving capitalist inequities at one point in time and challenging them at another. While sustained focus will enable deeper and more meaningful engagement with any one path, music educators and students will necessarily alter their choices in light of personal need and social circumstance. As such, the question is not whether to thrive, survive, resist, or challenge but rather *when* to engage in each of these practices.

In the spirit of *Choose Your Own Adventure* books, the following four chapters can be read in any order. To examine how music education can contribute to more equitable thriving within capitalist economies, continue to chapter 4. To consider more equitable surviving under capitalism, turn to chapter 5. To explore resisting capitalist inequities, read chapter 6, and to investigate directly challenging capitalist inequities, skip to chapter 7.

NOTES

1. Bennett Reimer, *A Philosophy of Music Education* (Hoboken, NJ: Prentice Hall, 1970).

2. David J. Elliott, *Music Matters: A New Philosophy of Music Education* (New York: Oxford University Press, 1995); David J. Elliott and Marissa Silverman, *Music Matters: A Philosophy of Music Education*, 2nd ed. (New York: Oxford University Press, 2015).

3. Gregory J. Seigworth and Melissa Gregg, "An Inventory of Shimmers," in *The Affect Theory Reader*, ed. Melissa Gregg and Gregory J. Seigworth (Durham, NC: Duke University Press, 2010), 1.

4. Brian Massumi, "The Autonomy of Affect," *Cultural Critique* 31 (1995): 84.

5. Massumi, "Autonomy of Affect," 84.

6. Massumi, "Autonomy of Affect," 85.

7. Massumi, "Autonomy of Affect," 85.

8. Massumi, "Autonomy of Affect," 86. In this instance, Massumi conflates *emotion* with *feeling*. Drawing on Antonio Damasio, I assert that *feeling* would be the more appropriate term, which is why I have used it in this sentence. Antonio R. Damasio, *The Feeling of What Happens: Body and Emotion in the Making of Consciousness* (Orlando: Harcourt, 1999).

9. Massumi, "Autonomy of Affect," 88.

10. For an extended discussion of emotions and feeling in music education, see Elliott and Silverman, *Music Matters*, 189.

11. Massumi, "Autonomy of Affect," 88.

12. Sianne Ngai, *Ugly Feelings* (Cambridge, MA: Harvard University Press, 2005), 27.

13. Ngai, *Ugly Feelings*, 35.

14. Seigworth and Gregg, "Inventory of Shimmers," 2.

15. Massumi, "Autonomy of Affect," 96.

16. Seigworth and Gregg, "Inventory of Shimmers," 2–3.

17. Hua Hsu, "That Feeling When: What Affect Theory Teaches about the New Age of Anxiety," *New Yorker*, March 25, 2019, 64.

18. Hsu, "That Feeling When," 62.

19. David Harvey, *A Companion to Marx's Capital: The Complete Edition* (Brooklyn: Verso Books, 2018), 90.

20. Arlie Hochschild, *Strangers in Their Own Land: Anger and Morning on the American Right* (New York: New Press, 2016), 136.

21. Hochschild, *Strangers in Their Own Land*, 136.

22. Hochschild, *Strangers in Their Own Land*, 136.

23. Karl Marx, "Estranged Labor," *Economic and Philosophical Manuscripts 1844*, accessed June 27, 2023, https://www.marxists.org/archive/marx/works/1844/manuscripts/labour.htm.

24. Michael J. Sandel, *The Tyranny of Merit: What's Become of the Common Good?* (New York: Farrar, Straus and Giroux, 2020), 27.

25. Alabama State Department of Education, "School District Per Pupil Expenditures FY 2022," accessed October 21, 2024. https://reportcard.alsde.edu/Docs/System_SchoolLevelPPE_FY2022.pdf.

26. Marx, "Estranged Labor."

27. Lizzie Davey, "How Much Does TikTok Pay Creators?" *Descript*, November 8, 2023, https://www.descript.com/blog/article/how-much-does-tiktok-pay.

28. Hartmut Rosa, *Resonance: A Sociology of Our Relationship to the World*, trans. James C. Wagner (Cambridge: Polity Press, 2019), 184.

29. Simon Kemp, "Digital 2022: Data Overview Report," *Data Reportal*, January 26, 2022, https://datareportal.com/reports/digital-2022-global-overview-report.

30. Noreena Hertz, *The Lonely Century: How to Restore Human Connection in a World That's Pulling Apart* (New York: Currency, 2021), 12.

31. Rosa, *Resonance*, 184.

32. Randall Allsup, *Remixing the Classroom* (Bloomington: Indiana University Press, 2016); Randall Allsup and Heidi Westerlund, "Methods and Situational Ethics in Music Education," *Action, Criticism, and Theory for Music Education* 11, no. 1 (2012): 124–48.

33. Lauren Kapalka Richerme, *Complicating, Considering, and Connecting Music Education* (Bloomington: Indiana University Press, 2020); Patrick Schmidt, "Ethics or Choosing Complexity in Music Relations," *Action, Criticism, and Theory for Music Education* 11, no. 1 (2012): 149–68.

34. See, for example, Marja Heimonen, "'Bildung' and Music Education: A Finnish Perspective," *Philosophy of Music Education Review* 22, no. 2 (2014): 188–208; Warner Jank, "Didaktik, Bildung, Content: On the Writings of Frede V. Nielsen," *Philosophy of Music Education Review* 22, no. 2 (2014): 113–31.

35. Nancy Fraser, *The Old Is Dying and the New Cannot Be Reborn* (Brooklyn: Verso Books, 2019).

36. See, for example, Warren N. Churchill and Cara Faith Bernard, "Disability and the Ideology of Ability: How Might Music Educators Respond?" *Philosophy of Music Education Review* 28, no. 1 (2020): 24–46; Elizabeth Gould, "Women Working in Music Education: The War Machine," *Philosophy of Music Education Review* 17, no. 2 (2009): 126–43; Joyce McCall, "'A Peculiar Sensation': Mirroring Du Bois' Path into Predominantly White Institutions in the 21st Century," *Action, Criticism, and Theory for Music Education* 20, no. 4 (2021): 10–44, https://doi.org/10.22176/act20.4.10.

37. Fraser, *Old Is Dying and the New Cannot Be Reborn*, 39–40.

38. Fraser, *Old Is Dying and the New Cannot Be Reborn*, 10.

39. Quentin Wheeler-Bell, "An Immanent Critique of Critical Pedagogy," *Educational Theory* 69, no. 3 (2019): 280.

40. Rosa, *Resonance*, 184. In music education, the term *resonant* has been associated with narrative research practices. There is overlap with Sandra Stauffer and Margaret Barrett's contention that resonant work "reverberates and resonates in and through the communities it serves" and Rosa's description of resonance as a vibratory wire involving adaptive transformation with the world. However, Stauffer and Barrett do not directly address the relationship between resonance and alienation or clarify how resonance can function as both a descriptive and normative concept. Sandra Stauffer and Margaret Barrett, "Narrative Inquiry in Music Education: Toward Resonant Work," in *Narrative Inquiry in Music Education: Troubling Certainty*, ed. Margaret Barrett and Sandra Stauffer (New York: Springer Science+Business Media, 2009).

41. Rosa, *Resonance*, 163.

42. Rosa, *Resonance*, 185.

43. Rosa, *Resonance*, 185.

44. Rosa, *Resonance*, 161.

45. Rosa, *Resonance*, 185.

46. Rosa, *Resonance*, 185.

47. Rosa, *Resonance*, 174.

48. Rosa, *Resonance*, 316.

49. Rosa, *Resonance*, 221.

50. Rosa, *Resonance*, 171.

51. Rosa, *Resonance*, 171.

52. Rosa, *Resonance*, 174.

53. In selecting this framing, I draw on and promote a commercial product created to benefit capitalist producers. While I acknowledge the limitations of this decision, I argue that the benefits—particularly the idea of reuse by returning again and again to the start of the book, which resists capitalist emphasis on single-use, disposable products—outweigh the drawbacks.

FOUR

THRIVING WITHIN CAPITALISM

From Competition to Monopolization

THRIVING WITHIN CAPITALISM HAS ONE criterion: making as much money as possible. According to the 2022 Credit Suisse Global Wealth Report, individuals with a net worth of over one million USD make up 1.2 percent of humanity,[1] including 84,490 adults with wealth above one hundred million USD.[2] Combined, this 1.2 percent accounts for 47.8 percent of global wealth.[3]

As detailed in chapter 1, contemporary capitalist economies rely on human and environmental exploitation, propagating unethical material inequities across the globe. Yet refraining from examining how individuals gain a position on the upper rungs of the capitalist pyramid reinforces the existing status quo of economic winners and losers. Since the highest rates of upward and downward mobility typically occur between the ages of twenty-five to thirty-five,[4] P-12 and collegiate education may play a role in providing knowledge and experiences beneficial for individuals aiming to improve their economic positionality.

Music education scholars have noted that long-standing practices such as competitions and standardization align with and reinforce neoliberal capitalist policies, benefiting those already at the top of the capitalist pyramid.[5] Alternatively, music educators have advocated for innovations, including relevant and flexible music education practices.[6] As detailed in chapter 2, relevant music making often fosters ongoing consumption, and flexibility enables precarious employment, so these practices also reinforce existing capitalist hierarchies. Yet philosophers have not examined what, if any, aspects of either long-standing or innovative music education practices might support students' thriving within capitalism.

Thriving within capitalism almost always necessitates some degree of luck: #soblessed. Seminal capitalist theorist Friedrich Hayek praised capitalism for not predestining individuals to certain occupations. However, he observed: "Even in the best of worlds this freedom will be very limited. Few people have ever an abundance of choice of occupation."[7] As such, not achieving a dream job or financial success may have more to do with chance than with one's skillset or work ethic.

Specifically, adults' economic positionalities are highly correlated with their birth circumstances. According to researchers at the Brookings Institution, those who start at the top of the capitalist pyramid have the greatest probability of remaining at the top.[8] As they summarize: "The most common ending quintile for those who start in the bottom quintile is still the bottom quintile."[9] While hard work can facilitate upward mobility—and laziness, downward mobility—luck plays an outsized role in economic success within capitalist systems.

Additionally, capitalist practices are continually changing and often place specific.[10] The knowledge and experiences that made someone a profitable leader in the eighteenth-century British East India Company, for example, contrast with those of a twenty-first-century Silicon Valley tech mogul. More broadly, Nancy Fraser notes that capitalism relies on historically situated struggles over boundaries, including between exploitation through low-wage labor and expropriation through confiscating humans' capacities and natural resources.[11] Few individuals have the luxury of being born at a time and place in which exploitation and expropriation do not severely limit or outright deny opportunities to thrive within capitalism.[12]

Furthermore, systematic institutional privileges and barriers make thriving within capitalism more likely for some individuals than others. Not only does the median white American start with thirteen times more wealth than the median Black American, but Black and white Americans who start with the same wealth in their early thirties will, on average, diverge financially. According to authors at the Brookings Institution,

> A white person in the 25th percentile of the wealth distribution in their early thirties is expected to move up to the 44th percentile by their late fifties, while a Black person who starts with the same wealth level will only move up to the 29th percentile, on average. Similarly, white Americans who start with high wealth (90th percentile) have much higher wealth in their late fifties (77th percentile) than Black Americans (51st percentile) who start with high wealth, on average. White Americans thus experience both more upward mobility and less downward mobility, in terms of wealth, than Black Americans.[13]

These disparities are neither random nor a product of luck. Rather, they result because systematic racism is key to capitalism.[14]

Likewise, individuals with disabilities are far more likely than those without disabilities to be unemployed and live in poverty, and women have significantly less wealth than men.[15] According to the American National Women's Law Center, "for every $1 of wealth owned by a single man, single women own 82 cents."[16] The intersection of race and gender creates even larger gaps. For every one dollar of wealth a white, single American male owns, single American Black and Latina women only own nine cents.[17]

While I want to stress the role of both luck and systematic oppression in determining who thrives under capitalism, adopting an attitude of defeatism reinforces current economic positionalities. As billionaire entrepreneur and PayPal cofounder Peter Thiel notes, "If you treat the future as something definite, it makes sense to understand it in advance and to work to shape it. But if you expect an indefinite future ruled by randomness, you'll give up on trying to master it."[18] By definition, pyramidal systems, including capitalism, necessitate that most individuals exist on the lowest rungs, but those who do not contemplate the skills and dispositions that support financial success have little hope of improving their starting economic positionality. Music educators might therefore acknowledge the improbability of class mobility while still assisting students interested in such a pursuit.

Given both the role of luck and the ever-evolving nature of capitalist accumulation processes, no writer can offer a definitive set of "how to thrive within capitalism" practices. Yet examining stories about and advice from contemporary individuals who have accumulated great wealth may provide insights and useful practices. Although this chapter includes references to key capitalist theories such as Hayek's, I center narratives from and about those currently thriving within contemporary capitalist systems. These include relatively privileged entrepreneurs like Sheryl Sandberg, who was born to educated parents and attended Ivy League schools, as well as entrepreneurs from historically marginalized communities, including musician Kendrick Lamar. In addition to experiencing racial discrimination, Lamar's parents were on and off welfare, and he lived in a violent neighborhood; according to Lamar's biographer, at ages five and eight, he witnessed people being gunned down.[19]

Since success narratives center economic winners, they do not fully address qualities that can undermine thriving within capitalism. Those who succeed within capitalist systems may also not possess a comprehensive understanding of the dispositions and actions that enabled their success. In particular, they may downplay or remain unaware of how socially shunned qualities, such as narcissism, deceitfulness, and a cutthroat mentality, contributed to their financial gains. As such, the values and practices presented in this chapter are necessary but almost certainly insufficient for thriving within capitalism.

I conclude the chapter with ideas for how music educators might promote more equitable thriving within capitalism. Yet as Sean Powell notes regarding music competitions, "breaking down barriers so that all can have access to an unfair system is not justice."[20] Providing students a more equitable chance to thrive under capitalism does not alter the unethical exploitation on which contemporary globalized capitalism relies.

CONTINUAL IMPROVEMENT

Many people work diligently their entire lives and never accumulate wealth, and educators should understand the limits of focusing on merit rather than the common good.[21] However, most individuals who thrive within capitalism exhibit the qualities of hard work and determination. Sandberg describes constantly asking herself, "How can I improve?" as well as setting personal goals for what new skills she could learn every eighteen months.[22] Similarly, Lamar's biographer describes him as a "perfectionist" and "not one to be defeated by hard work."[23]

Although few teachers would claim not to value students' hard work, there is a difference between making continued improvement a primary value versus one of many aims. Regardless of the musical genre or practice, a music educator devoted to developing students' work ethic would constantly set individualized goals and assess students' progress toward them.[24] They would encourage students to meet preset standards with little care for extenuating circumstances or individual hardships. While students' interests could play a role in such processes, achievement would take precedence over personal joy or fulfillment.

Importantly, students would focus their hard work and determination on building deep expertise. Unfocused hard work encourages diffuse results, making it difficult to distinguish one hard worker from another. Thiel argues that "instead of pursuing many-sided mediocrity and calling it 'well-roundedness,'" individuals should determine "the one best thing to do" and then work tirelessly at it.[25] Rather than aiming for broad musical knowledge and flexible musicianship, thriving-focused music educators would encourage students to distinguish themselves within a single skill area.

Within areas of specialization, competitive comparisons typically drive the work ethic of those thriving within capitalism. Lamar's biographer explains: "He didn't just want to get by, he wanted to be the best, and that meant tapping into a level of focus he hadn't before. It meant pouring everything into his creative being and doing what he could to protect it."[26] Music educators seeking to develop competitiveness might emphasize the importance of beating others through chair placements, competitions for solos, and public displays of achievement such as star charts, certificates, and trophies. They might center solo and ensemble competitions with other schools while avoiding a "we're all winners" mentality. In addition to favoring types of music making with extensive preexisting competitions, they could create rigorous competitions for classes without widespread contest opportunities, such as songwriting or ukulele.

Although procapitalist author Ayn Rand attributes competitive success solely to individuals' talents and work ethic,[27] accounts of contemporary financially successful individuals acknowledge how constructive feedback from others contributed to achievement. For example, Moore details how Lamar's seventh-grade English teacher Regis Inge "didn't take it easy on him. When Kendrick submitted his work in school, Inge would often send it back with visible prompts for the budding poet to dig deeper. Basic language wouldn't cut it; the young man needed to strengthen his lexicon before his prose could truly shine."[28] Providing meaningful feedback necessitates that music educators have deep familiarity with the practices in which students specialize. Ideally, teachers wishing to support students' thriving within capitalism should only facilitate music making they feel comfortable critiquing at a high level.

In addition to benefiting from unsolicited mentor advice, those who thrive within capitalism report continually seeking out critical observation. Sandberg recounts consistently soliciting feedback about her weaknesses, noting that "the upside of painful knowledge is so much greater than the downside of blissful ignorance."[29] Similarly, computer scientist and cofounder of Pixar Ed Catmull argues that successful businesses necessitate a culture in which all employees feel free to share their honest appraisals.[30] While music educators should not misuse the free labor of others, they might have students practice asking for feedback from those with more expertise—perhaps classmates, local solo performers, or members of an online video-game music community. Teachers and students might use this information to construct ambitious, individualized, measurable goals.

Hard work, competition, and constructive feedback can contribute to thriving within capitalism, but in isolation these qualities encourage replication, which undermines financial success. When a glut of highly trained instrumentalists uses the same repertoire to compete for a single spot in a major symphony orchestra, orchestra leaders have little incentive to raise musicians' salaries. Likewise, when neighboring music organizations program similar events, they must minimize prices or risk losing their limited audience base to competitors.

Thiel describes capitalism and competition as opposites. He explains: "Capitalism is premised on the accumulation of capital, but under perfect competition all profits get competed away."[31] Similarly, David Harvey argues that while key capitalist theorists Adam Smith and Karl Marx accepted competition "as gospel," monopolies are foundational to capitalism.[32]

Harvey traces monopolization to early capitalist practices. Since one factory cannot exist physically atop another, "an advantageous location (with privileged access to transport links, resources or markets) gives me a certain monopoly power in competition with others."[33] Likewise, contemporary capitalists like Thiel encourage entrepreneurs to seek out monopolistic positions in which their company alone serves a particular market segment.[34] It follows that high-quality artistic replication may provide initial accolades, but intense competition within preestablished boundaries inhibits opportunities for students to distinguish themselves in the longer term.

FROM COMPETITION TO MONOPOLIZATION

Rather than winning within existing markets, those who accumulate the greatest amount of wealth within contemporary capitalism often change the very nature of the capitalist playing field. Touting their "blue oceans" strategy, in which entrepreneurs look for untapped markets while avoiding saturated "red oceans," business leaders W. Chan Kim and Renée Mauborgne argue that companies should avoid understanding competition to preset industry standards as a benchmark.[35] Likewise, Lamar's biographer observes that Lamar initially "had all the technical prowess, the complex sentence structures, and the natural cadence, but he didn't sound free.... He wasn't playing the long game yet. He hadn't realized that the truest path to immortality was to be his fully authentic self."[36]

Monopoly formation begins by considering what sets one's product apart from others' contributions. For example, rather than trying to compete directly with existing airline carriers, Southwest diverged by aiming to attract people who traveled by bus, train, and car on short-haul trips.[37] By focusing on low prices and frequent departures while avoiding investments in meals, lounges, and seating choices—which nonair transportation also lacked—Southwest reshaped the airline industry.[38] Innovating in ways that altered industry conditions enabled Southwest to dominate its newly created market.[39]

Similarly, when highly skilled music makers develop a unique artistic voice, they create and thus monopolize a new market segment without fear of competition. For example, consider how the unique theatrics of classical pianists Lang Lang and Yuja Wang set them apart from their more restrained contemporaries.

Rather than competing directly with the musical mastery of performers like András Schiff and Mitsuko Uchida, Lang and Wang created new market sections for audiences that valued visual engagement alongside high-level classical music making. They therefore enticed individuals uninterested in traditional classical piano concerts to attend their events. In Thiel's terms, these music makers became "creative monopolists," providing customers choices "by adding entirely new categories of abundance to the world."[40]

Given the importance of uniqueness in creative monopolies, it is unsurprising that successful capitalist entrepreneurs often note the diverse and at times interdisciplinary nature of their work. For example, rather than primarily pursuing computer science and technology classes in college, former Apple CEO and billionaire Steve Jobs took pleasure in following his curiosities, including by taking a calligraphy class.[41] Likewise, Lamar studied music from various cultures, comparing it with his own self-expression "to strengthen his art."[42] When combined with high-level achievement and a competitive mindset, divergent thinking can set individuals apart from competitors.

Table 1 illuminates how rigorous skill development intersects with the uniqueness of musical practices. Music educators and students aiming to thrive within capitalism could focus on the monopolistic upper-right quadrant, which combines deep learning in a single music style or genre with opportunities for individual distinction. For example, they might balance high-level skill attainment on an individual instrument or software platform with opportunities for songwriting, multimedia projects, or other unique and perhaps interdisciplinary musical endeavors. Given that more globally popular genres like rock and hip-hop have the potential to reach a wider audience—and thus create more profit—than classical and jazz music practices, thriving-focused music educators would foreground advanced skill development in those more lucrative areas.

Table 4.1 Skill level versus standardization

	Preset standards	**Unique**
Deep skills	Classes with long-standing methods and/or competitions (e.g., Kodály and Orff; traditional band, choir, and orchestra practices)	Monopoly = sequential classes enabling both sustained skill development and creativity/ interdisciplinarity
Minimal or diffuse skills	Short term electives based on replication (e.g., one semester of modern band)	Short term electives based on self-expression (e.g., single songwriting class)

Table 1 also underscores how the combination of uniqueness and high-level musical skill necessary for monopolization contrasts with pervasive music education practices. The upper-left quadrant involves the mixing of high-level musical skill and preset forms of evaluation; this combination typically occurs in both sequential general music classes and traditional band, choir, and orchestra settings. The solo and ensemble competitions that accompany traditional band, choir, and orchestra classes create situations in which students focus on beating their rivals, thus mirroring organizations that become obsessed with marketplace competitors. In Thiel's words: "Rivalry causes us to overemphasize old opportunities and slavishly copy what has worked in the past."[43] Music education competitions centered on a single style or practice can serve an important role in deepening students' work ethic and expertise, but because ratings on preset rubrics restrict opportunities for innovation that might trouble and transcend existing evaluative criteria, they undermine the conditions needed for creative monopoly formation.

Alternatively, the more accessible music education practices found on the bottom row of table 1 do not provide students the skills needed to distinguish themselves from their peers. In the bottom-right quadrant, students develop individual forms of musical expression through classes such as a one-semester songwriting or video-game music course. Students might find such music making personally fulfilling, but it will not encourage them to achieve a level of artistic expertise that sets them apart from countless other hobbyists. However, in the absence of sequential, creative monopoly–focused classes, electives foregrounding unique musical expressivity could complement standardized high-level musical achievement typical within traditional band, choir, and orchestra classes. Adding these classes to existing ensemble-based music education programs could foster skills and dispositions needed for creative monopoly formation.

Practices in the lower-left quadrant involve both minimal musical skills and the repetition of previous standards. These might include music appreciation classes or single semester electives focused on replicating existing songs, such as a rock band or a hip-hop class. Although potentially valuable for other reasons, such endeavors foster neither the depth of study nor the individuality important for creating an artistic monopoly.

While a necessary prerequisite for thriving within capitalism, sustained, single-minded focus on unique skill development does not always result in creation of a monopolistic space. Catmull explains that original thinking is fragile and necessitates continual refinement to produce marketable artistic content.[44] He summarizes: "Creative people must accept that challenges never cease, failure can't be avoided, and 'vision' is often an illusion."[45] Developing creative monopolies therefore takes not just skill and individuality but also a tolerance for significant risk and repeated failure. As such, individuals who thrive within capitalism explain resilience as key to their financial success.[46]

In addition to promoting the development of high-level skills in unique artistic areas, music educators aiming to promote thriving within capitalism might consider how risk and failure play out in their classroom. Do they reward students more for bold uncertainty or predictable replication? Do they demonstrate taking substantial artistic risks and allow students to witness their responses to failure? How do they facilitate the resiliency of students who flounder in the process of taking significant risks?

Taking bold risks can involve expanding the reach of one's artistic endeavors. The more people one's music making impacts, the more potential financial gain is at stake. Thiel explains: "A monopoly business gets stronger as it gets bigger."[47] Expansive affective flows may play a role in such growth.

EXPANSIVE AFFECTIVE FLOWS

In artistic experiences, expansion can involve intensifying affects. Just as angry social media posts get shared more often than calm ones, more intense artistic experiences have greater potential to excite participants, thus expanding the reach of such music making.[48] For example, imagine a marching band holding the final chord of a football halftime show as the drum major turns to the crowd and incites continued applause. The drum major then turns to the band and has it increase the volume of the chord. As the intensity flows outward from the ensemble, members of the crowd rise to their feet in excitement.

Across many music genres and practices, participants' affective experiences intensify through an increase in tempo and dynamic level. Whether a waltz that speeds up, a jazz improvisation with quickening arpeggios, or a rap song with accented lyrics, affective intensity builds through fastness and loudness. Consider this poetic demonstration:

Beat,   pause,   beat, Beat
The angry tweet,   the frustrated child
Blood boils, Runs hot
Blazing, searing, torrid
Quick, quicker, **Bold,** BIG
Agitate, churn, disturb, Rouse
Accelerating EXCITEMENT
Faster-FASTER, Rapid, Racing
PRESTO-hold-HOLD—**HOLD!**; cut

As intensity increases, participants become ever-more drawn into the artistic endeavor. Music makers can use this captured attention to seek added financial compensation for their work. For example, the marching band director could ask the excited crowd to donate money, or a thrilling online music video could end with a link to purchase recordings, merchandise, or a subscription service.

In addition to captivating participants, intensifying affective experiences have the potential to reach those on the periphery of an event. If you read the above poetic writing while seated next to someone engaged in another activity, your own increased heart rate may impact their experience. Likewise, the loudening marching band performance may reach game attendees initially unaware of or uninterested in the halftime show, potentially creating new fans and consumers. Yet increases in speed and volume cannot continue indefinitely. While faster tempos and louder dynamics may create momentarily expansive affective flows, ongoing capitalist expansion ultimately necessitates an ever-growing group of potential consumers to engage with such music making.

The quality of artistic experiences often plays a role in their potential influence, but it is not the only consideration. Hayek noted that capitalist compensation derives from the "usefulness" of a trade "to other members of society, even if this should stand in no relation to subjective merit."[49] Regardless of whether most individuals with music performance degrees deem Mitsuko Uchida's or Yuja Wang's piano playing superior, Uchida and Wang ultimately receive compensation based on how many and how much consumers pay to hear them. Rather than relying on professionally agreed-on merit, using music making to thrive within capitalism involves one's ability to expand affective reach. This is not to imply that Wang's artistry is solely motivated by economic concerns. Rather, culture continually evolves, and music industry leaders play a primary role in highlighting that evolution for financial gains.

Key nineteenth- and twentieth-century American music educators like Lowell Mason and John Philip Sousa thrived financially through showy performances for broad audiences, yet few contemporary music educators seek out widespread community engagement. Parents and friends of participating students constitute the majority of attendees at most music education performances, and teachers rarely make an effort to expand this customer base. Outside of school concerts, music students perform at competitions, in which rival competitors and supporters constitute the audience. Although ensembles may occasionally perform at sporting events and town ceremonies or parades, these activities often fulfill a duty rather than strategically expand music makers' circle of influence.

Alternatively, providing musical experiences that football enthusiasts or other populations largely uninterested in traditional school concerts or competitions might value could expand the reach of artists. As Kim and Mauborgne note, successful capitalists do not just focus on better serving a specific limited buyer group; they also redefine and grow the buyer group for a given industry.[50] Redefining the marching band buyer group as football enthusiasts rather than band parents and a few judges enables music educators and students to select music making that best serves those more numerous individuals' desires.

Importantly, those who thrive within capitalism typically start by aiming to capture a sizable share of a particular market rather than trying to reach all potential consumers at once. Thiel explains that since monopolies by definition dominate a large market share, start-ups should begin with small, specific groups of consumers.[51] For example, rather than starting with all football fans, music makers might focus on expanding affective flows to reach older community members who regularly attend school sporting events.

In addition to asking what music making potential consumers might value, music educators and students aiming to thrive within capitalism would market to those individuals. Thiel exposes the myth that products sell themselves, asserting: "If you've invented something new but you haven't invented an effective way to sell it, you have a bad business—no matter how good the product."[52] Likewise, even the most skillful, innovative, and intense artistic endeavors necessitate a plan for reaching an ever-expanding group of potential customers. Such marketing might include social media campaigns, advertisements, personal invitations, and collaborations with other organizations. Yet guessing or reasoning about what music making certain individuals might value does not guarantee success. As entrepreneurs Steve Blank and Bob Dorf note, "No business plan survives first contact with customers."[53]

As such, those aiming to thrive within capitalism continually evaluate customers' experiences. Founder of multiple successful start-ups Eric Ries explains that such organizations constantly measure how customers respond to products and pivot quickly when needed.[54] In addition to observing audience members' in-the-moment responses, music educators and students trying to please a specific segment of the football crowd could have informal conversations with those individuals and use surveys to evaluate their impact. They could then brainstorm about how to increase their usefulness to those consumers and adapt their music-making practices accordingly.

Yet experiences consumers find highly engaging can still become uninteresting over time. Ongoing change and adaptation play a key role in maintaining dominance within creative markets.[55] In considering how to capture and maintain audiences' attention, business scholars Chip and Dan Heath propose the principle of unexpectedness.[56] They elaborate: "We need to violate people's expectations. We need to be counterintuitive."[57] Expansive affective flows might therefore involve not just intensity but also the surprise needed to maintain consumers' interest. They could

Pivot
shake, pulse, find, seek
compete, win, win, NOW
buy, own, dominate
SUR
P
RI
SE
          EXPE
Ctations
pulse, Pulse, plus, add
free market; free dom
pi   VoT
                                                                                    Consume Backward
Extract-Expand
Quicker! Better!
P   iv   OT
                              Expected (UN)
                                                  PIVOT Again

There's (always) more . . .

Thus far I have argued that thriving within capitalism necessitates hard work, a competitive disposition, and risk. Yet rather than competing with direct rivals, capitalists aim to build monopolies, which rely on combining high-level skills with unique innovation. Monopolies survive only through ongoing growth, which may involve intense, expansive affective flows responsive and adaptive to customers' needs. In short, Art becomes ART becomes #art, #a$t, and @$+.[58]

However, the capitalist playing field is highly uneven; those beginning with fewer material resources remain far less likely to ever thrive. Absent added consideration, the aforementioned thriving practices will further existing material inequities. Moreover, since music educators can only facilitate the thriving of students they teach, the overrepresentation of higher socioeconomic students in secondary school elective music classes undermines opportunities for more equitable thriving within capitalism.[59] How might thriving-focused music educators work against such tendencies?

MORE EQUITABLE THRIVING WITHIN CAPITALISM

In addition to calling for more equitable funding across schools, music educators might examine how their own policies deter students from lower socioeconomic class backgrounds from participating in music electives or becoming top achievers within mandatory general music courses.[60] Students' musical interests may also play a role in their decision to elect or excel within music study. As Vincent Bates observes, students with lower socioeconomic class backgrounds often want to play instruments like guitar and engage in genres of music such as country, underrepresented within formal music education.[61]

Music educators might address students' divergent interests by emphasizing deep musical skill development that transfers across genres. Since learning various scales and chords by ear promotes more cross-genre facility than learning songs via Western notation, early instruction might emphasize aural learning, perhaps with an elective option for Western notation in later study. Given that more robust thriving within capitalism ultimately involves creating a new monopolistic position, music educators might encourage students—particularly those with lower socioeconomic class backgrounds—to focus on interdisciplinary artistic engagements. The significant role Lamar's seventh-grade English teacher played in his poetic development illustrates how educators in other subjects may have expertise on which music educators can draw.

Since thriving within capitalism involves developing a competitive mindset, music educators might ensure that lower socioeconomic class students have opportunities to compete. Traditional solo and ensemble festivals often involve time and financial commitments that can exclude lower socioeconomic class students, so teachers might focus on within-school competitions as well as cross-school virtual competitions. Music educators might also devise competitions that look beyond standardized forms of musical achievement. Perhaps students compete to get the most downloads of a newly composed song or the highest ratings from community members on metrics important for commercial success, such as enjoyment and interest. Given that a key part of capitalist thriving involves developing consumers, music educators could consider providing students from lower socioeconomic class households added input in determining which consumer base the class or ensemble targets, how it does so, and how to evaluate their efforts.

Few accounts of successful entrepreneurs dive deeply into issues of copyright, likely because such individuals employ lawyers to manage their intellectual property. Yet protecting one's artistic or other potentially monopolistic ideas is a key concern for beginning entrepreneurs. At present, many music makers freely post their work on platforms such as TikTok absent any compensation. Since students from high socioeconomic class backgrounds typically have more access to lawyers than those from lower socioeconomic class backgrounds, teaching knowledge about and experience with copyright processes may promote more equitable thriving within capitalism. Music educators and students might also keep updated on potentially lucrative forms of intellectual property ownership, such as nonfungible tokens (NFTs). Demystifying such forms of ownership by experimenting with them as a class can serve as an important model for students' future capitalist endeavors.

Additionally, given that those starting with fewer financial resources often face added traumas because of their material circumstances, promoting their thriving within capitalism necessitates supporting their holistic well-being. This support might include providing information about counseling and social services as well as mindfulness and other forms of wellness enhancement. While music educators should not offer guidance about areas outside of their professional expertise, they can encourage struggling students to seek appropriate support.

Thriving within capitalism ultimately involves great risk, and students from lower socioeconomic class backgrounds may wish to exchange more modest financial gains for job security. Given current teacher shortages and the relative stability of employment within P-12 schools, this tradeoff might include pursuing music teacher licensure. In order to promote more equitable access to undergraduate music education degrees, collegiate schools of music need to make their admission processes and programs at large more welcoming for students from lower socioeconomic class backgrounds. Joseph Abramo and Cara Bernard found that such action might involve eliminating the requirement of private lessons, being more inclusive of community music making, and reconsidering nonmusic entrance requirements.[62] Additionally, secondary music educators can assist lower socioeconomic class students by demystifying the audition process, including through putting interested students in touch with local music education professors.

Music educators at all levels might consider how underrepresented musical instruments and practices can provide opportunities for monopolistic skill development. For example, high-achieving bassoonists, horn players, violists, and tenor and bass singers often have an easier time gaining college scholarships and admission to music schools than pianists, violinists, and soprano vocalists. As such, music educators might encourage students with fewer financial resources to consider less competitive areas of music study. However, since collegiate music study rarely facilitates students' mobility into upper classes, teachers might also point students with good grades seeking financial stability toward more lucrative professions, such as computer science, law, and medicine.

Ultimately, more equitable capitalist thriving necessitates policies that enable individuals with few financial resources to take thoughtful risks without fear of lifelong destitution. While Hayek derided broad-based forms of social welfare, he advocated for government policies ensuring that those who earnestly tried but failed to achieve financial success receive "adequate security against severe privation."[63] Supporting policies, such as universal healthcare, that enable individuals without family wealth to risk enacting what could become lucrative ideas is key to more equitable thriving within capitalism.

In summary, as members of contemporary globalized capitalist economies, it is important that music educators consider how their practices might contribute to thriving within capitalism, particularly for those currently on the bottom of inequitable capitalist pyramids. The absence of such thinking reinforces the socioeconomic status quo. However, since only a small number of individuals ultimately thrive within capitalism, and a single-minded focus on thriving necessitates foregoing other, perhaps more personally meaningful artistic opportunities, music educators and students might simultaneously consider other paths forward.

In the spirit of *Choose Your Own Adventure* books, continue onto chapter 5 to find an examination of playfully surviving under capitalism. Alternatively, to explore resisting capitalist inequities, turn to chapter 6; and to investigate directly challenging capitalist inequities, skip to chapter 7.

NOTES

1. Credit Suisse Research Institute, "Global Wealth Report 2022," *Credit Suisse*, accessed August 27, 2024, https://www.credit-suisse.com/about-us/en/reports-research/studies-publications.html#:~:text=The%20Global%20wealth%20report%202018&text=During%20the%20twelve%20months%20to,high%20of%20%2463%2C100%20per%20adult, 21.
2. Credit Suisse Research Institute, "Global Wealth Report 2022," 28.
3. Credit Suisse Research Institute, "Global Wealth Report 2022," 21.
4. Ariel Gelrud Shiro, Christopher Pulliam, John Sabelhaus, and Ember Smith, "Stuck on the Ladder: Intergenerational Wealth Mobility in the United

States," *Brookings Institute*, June 2022, https://www.brookings.edu/wp-content/uploads/2022/06/2022_FMCI_IntragenerationalWealthMobility_FINAL.pdf, 5.

5. See, for example, Jess Mullen, "Music Education for Some: Music Standards at the Nexus of Neoliberal Reforms and Neoconservative Values," *Action, Criticism, and Theory for Music Education* 18, no. 1 (2019): 44–67; Sean Robert Powell, "Competition, Ideology, and the One-Dimensional Music Program," *Action, Criticism, and Theory for Music Education* 20, no. 3 (2021): 19–43.

6. See, for example, Randall Allsup, *Remixing the Classroom* (Bloomington: Indiana University Press, 2016), 14; Patricia Shehan Campbell, David Myers, and Ed Sarath, "Transforming Music Study from Its Foundations: A Manifesto for Progressive Change in the Undergraduate Preparation of Music Majors," *College Music Society*, 2016, https://www.music.org/pdf/pubs/tfumm/TFUMM.pdf, 1.

7. Friedrich A. Hayek, *The Road to Serfdom* (New York: Routledge, 1941), 97–98.

8. Gelrud Shiro, Pulliam, Sabelhaus, and Smith, "Stuck on the Ladder," 5.

9. Gelrud Shiro, Pulliam, Sabelhaus, and Smith, "Stuck on the Ladder," 16.

10. David Harvey, *Seventeen Contradictions and the End of Capitalism* (New York: Oxford University Press, 2014), 146–63.

11. Nancy Fraser, *Cannibal Capitalism: How Our System Is Devouring Democracy, Care, and the Planet—and What We Can Do about It* (Brooklyn: Verso Books, 2022), 20.

12. Fraser, *Cannibal Capitalism*, 20.

13. Gelrud Shiro, Pulliam, Sabelhaus, and Smith, "Stuck on the Ladder," 5.

14. See, for example, Fraser, *Cannibal Capitalism*, 27–52.

15. American Psychological Association, "Disability and Socioeconomic Status," accessed June 27, 2023, https://www.apa.org/pi/ses/resources/publications/disability.

16. National Women's Law Center, "Gender and Racial Wealth Gaps and Why They Matter," accessed June 27, 2023, https://nwlc.org/resource/gender-and-racial-wealth-gaps-and-why-they-matter/.

17. National Woman's Law Center, "Gender and Racial Wealth Gaps."

18. Peter Thiel, *Zero to One: Notes on Startups, or How to Build the Future*, ed. Blake Masters (New York: Crown Business, 2014), 55.

19. Marcus J. Moore, *The Butterfly Effect: How Kendrick Lamar Ignited the Soul of Black America* (Miami: Atria Books, 2020), 33–35.

20. Sean Robert Powell, *The Ideology of Competition in School Music* (New York: Oxford University Press, 2023), 111.

21. See, for example, Michael Sandel, *The Tyranny of Merit: What's Become of the Common Good?* (New York: Farrer, Straus and Giroux, 2020).

22. Sheryl Sandberg, *Lean In: Women, Work, and the Will to Lead*, ed. Nell Scovell (New York: Alfred A. Knopf, 2013), 52.

23. Moore, *Butterfly Effect*, 37, 70–71.

24. Such practices align with what Carol Dweck calls a growth mindset. Carol Dweck, *Self-Theories* (Lillington, NC: Taylor & Francis, 2000).

25. Thiel, *Zero to One*, 55.

26. Moore, *Butterfly Effect*, 37.

27. Ayn Rand, *Atlas Shrugged* (New York: Signet, 1996); Ayn Rand, *The Fountainhead* (New York: Signet, 1971).

28. Moore, *Butterfly Effect*, 37.

29. Sandberg, *Lean In*, 71.

30. Ed Catmull, *Creativity, Inc.: Overcoming the Unseen Forces That Stand in the Way of True Inspiration*, ed. Amy Wallace (New York: Random House, 2014), 14.

31. Thiel, *Zero to One*, 24.

32. Harvey, *Seventeen Contradictions and the End of Capitalism*, 132–34.

33. Harvey, *Seventeen Contradictions and the End of Capitalism*, 137.

34. Thiel, *Zero to One*, 24.

35. W. Chan Kim and Renée Mauborgne, *Blue Ocean Strategy Reader* (Boston: Harvard Business Review Press, 2014).

36. Moore, *Butterfly Effect*, 39–40.

37. Kim and Mauborgne, *Blue Ocean Strategy Reader*, 83.

38. Kim and Mauborgne, *Blue Ocean Strategy Reader*, 95–96.

39. Kim and Mauborgne, *Blue Ocean Strategy Reader*, 95–96.

40. Thiel, *Zero to One*, 31.

41. Walter Isaacson, *Steve Jobs* (New York: Simon & Schuster, 2011), 62.

42. Moore, *Butterfly Effect*, 37.

43. Thiel, *Zero to One*, 36.

44. Catmull, *Creativity, Inc.*, 108.

45. Catmull, *Creativity, Inc.*, 216.

46. See, for example, Steve Blank and Bob Dorf, *The Startup Owner's Manual: The Step-by-Step Guide for Building a Great Company* (Pescadero, CA: K & S Ranch, 2012), 47; Sandberg, *Lean In*, 53–55.

47. Thiel, *Zero to One*, 46.

48. David Nield, "Social Media Is Training Us to Unleash More Moral Outrage and Vitriol, Study Reveals," *Science Alert*, August 16, 2021, https://www.sciencealert.com/social-media-networks-are-training-us-to-express-more-outrage-online.

49. Hayak, *Road to Serfdom*, 126.

50. Kim and Mauborgne, *Blue Ocean Strategy Reader*, 66.

51. Thiel, *Zero to One*, 48.

52. Thiel, *Zero to One*, 121.

53. Blank and Dorf, *Startup Owner's Manual*, 46.

54. Eric Ries, *The Lean Startup: How Today's Startups Use Continuous Innovation to Create Radically Successful Businesses* (New York: Crown Business, 2011), 9.

55. Catmull, *Creativity, Inc.*, 120.

56. Chip Heath and Dan Heath, *Made to Stick: Why Some Ideas Survive and Others Die* (New York: Random House, 2007), 22.

57. Heath and Heath, *Made to Stick*, 22.

58. The capitalized ART is meant to indicate the bold intensity of expansive affective flows. The ideas of a$t and @$+ came from Indiana University graduate student Aaron Wonson.

59. Kenneth Elpus and Carlos R. Abril, "Who Enrolls in High School Music? A National Profile of U.S. Students, 2009–2013," *Journal of Research in Music Education* 67, no. 3 (2019): 323–38.

60. See further discussion about these barriers in the material equity section of chapter 3.

61. Vincent Bates, "Sustainable School Music for Poor, White, Rural Students," *Action, Criticism, and Theory for Music Education* 10, no. 2 (2011): 100–27, http://act.maydaygroup.org/articles/Bates10_2.pdf.

62. Joseph R. Abramo and Cara Faith Bernard, "Barriers to Access and University Schools of Music: A Collective Case Study of Urban High School Students of Color and Their Teachers," *Bulletin of the Council for Research in Music Education* 226 (2020): 7–26.

63. Hayek, *Road to Serfdom*, 137.

FIVE

SURVIVING CAPITALIST ALIENATION THROUGH PLAYFUL COMPOSING

CENTRAL TO HUMAN EXISTENCE IS surviving by adapting to present circumstances. While surviving entails obtaining necessities like food, water, and shelter, rising rates of drug overdoses and suicides in the United States and other wealthy capitalist countries demonstrate that humans need more than basic subsistence. Individuals throughout the world choose to make music in their leisure time, but music making alone does not necessarily enhance one's prospects for surviving under capitalist systems. As argued throughout this text, music educators can promote or demote values and practices that reinforce capitalism and its resultant vast material inequities.

Most individuals can take steps to improve their chances of thriving within capitalism, but the pyramidal structure on which capitalism depends demands that few be born into thriving circumstances—and even fewer transcend their inherited positionalities to markedly improve their financial status. Since those pursuing undergraduate music education degrees tend to come from economically stable households,[1] they may have the time and energy necessary to resist and challenge problematic aspects of contemporary capitalist practices. However, given the correlation between money and political power, a typical music educator's meager income may limit their impact, particularly given the increasing concentration of money and power among a small global elite.[2] Music educators may also face repercussions, including terminated employment, should they overtly challenge capitalism. Additionally, focusing on how students can work against capitalist ills may result in the omission of opportunities for learning skills and dispositions that could contribute to more robust personal fulfillment within capitalist systems.

Alongside examining the possibilities of thriving within, resisting, and challenging capitalism, educators and students might consider how music making can enhance their survival under capitalism. As detailed below, I understand survival-focused music education as involving resonant composing and playful affects. In contrast with thriving-focused music teachers and students, those emphasizing survival are unconcerned with reaping economic benefits from their endeavors, including in the form of self-promotion or group accolades. Since survival-focused music educators and students refuse to reinforce contemporary capitalist dispositions, their actions can be understood as a form of resistance. However, music educators and students attending to survival do not directly concern themselves with trying to resist or challenge capitalist ills; any undermining of capitalist ills is a byproduct of their focus on individually and collectively meaningful music making rather than a direct goal.

In addition to material inequities, over which individuals may have minimal control, what inhibits more robust surviving within contemporary capitalist systems? As detailed in chapter 3, alienation is a pervasive problem in capitalist societies. For Karl Marx, capitalist workers are alienated because stratified, largely immobile class divides inhibit them from both determining the terms of their employment and reaping the full financial rewards of their labor.[3] Limited in creativity and freedom, alienated workers produce profits for the capitalist upper class.

While P-12 students may not have experienced alienated work directly, formal schooling typically involves similar kinds of alienation. Schooling often occurs apart from community life, including local music making. Additionally, by relying on divides such as rigid bell schedules, separated seating arrangements, and constant teacher surveillance, contemporary education environments often parallel industrial workplaces.[4] In music education, alienation can occur through repetitive methodological practices, including formulaic use of Orff, Kodály, or other methodologies.[5] Focusing on the same inputs, such as daily scale exercises, and predetermined outputs, such as playing or singing test results and adjudicated festival scores, mirrors the separated, automatized processes of alienation key to capitalist laboring. Like laborers concentrated on receiving their next paycheck, students who aim to earn extrinsic rewards for learning musical skills separate the work of music making from intrinsic interest and leisurely enjoyment.

More broadly, Jacques Attali details the parallel between repetitive music making and capitalism.[6] In prior generations, musical engagements centered largely on the performance of new material composed for specific functions, such as church services.[7] However, beginning in the early twentieth century, music broadcasting and recording have enabled the easy consumption of previously composed music,[8] with producers selling identical copies of music recordings to the wider public. Just as mass production practices led to the consumption of identical rather than individually crafted commodities during the Industrial Revolution, individuals increasingly consume mass-produced music, which Attali argues furthers alienation.[9]

In addition to resisting alienating processes within music education, survival-focused music educators might facilitate students' development of skills and dispositions that counter the alienation they currently face within school and community environments and will likely face as capitalist workers. Extending the work of Attali, I begin by proposing that the aim of resonant composing might counter capitalist alienation. Subsequently, I explore how playful affective flows might encourage more robust and meaningful survival for individuals living within capitalist systems. In exploring possibilities for how artistic endeavors might contribute to more meaningful survival under capitalism, I at times break from scholarly writing conventions to experiment with survival-focused poetic expression.

RESONANT COMPOSING

Attali proposes composition as a possible alternative to the alienation of repetitive, mass-produced music recordings.[10] He explains composition as "inventing new codes" that create "our own relation with the world."[11] Rather than an escape or negation of lived circumstances, composing fosters a temporary sense of liberation within them.[12]

For example, in the American folk tune "The Hammer Song," Pete Seeger and Lee Hays created a code to express the ideals of comradery and justice.[13] Through the percussive guitar strumming, upbeat chord progression, and lyrics pairing the common worker's tool of a hammer with "love . . . all over this land," the composers sought not to resist laboring but to appropriate its tools for the fostering of communal joy. This emphasis on inventing relations with the world shares similarities with Hartmut Rosa's conception of resonance.[14] When music makers vibrate with and through their local environments, as opposed to vibrating at them in a self-focused way, they form meaningful resonances with those people and places.

Attali clarifies that rather than seeking affirmation from others, which would reinforce aspects of capitalist branding, composing involves collaboratively created communication. Through composing, individuals "hear the noises of others in exchange for one's own, to create, in common, the code within which communication will take place."[15] For instance, the pairing of music and visual images in compositions like Beyoncé's "Formation" invents codes that communicate communal anger at inequitable government responses to disasters—in this case, Hurricane Katrina. In Rosa's terms, such composing involves the transformative adaptation to and with one's surroundings key to resonance.[16]

Given the distinction made between composing, performing, and listening or responding in various contemporary music standards documents,[17] readers might initially understand composing as solely referencing the creation of new music. However, Attali specifically notes that listening can involve composing. He argues that "to listen to music in the network of composition is to rewrite it."[18] For example, imagine a participant with limited physical mobility engaging with Terence Blanchard's opera *Fire Shut Up in My Bones*, which tells the story of a financially impoverished young man traumatized by sexual abuse. While the participant may never have directly experienced poverty or sexual abuse, they might understand the protagonist's trauma and hardships through their own experiences with discrimination. As such, the participant in part rewrites the opera. While Blanchard composed the opera, performers and listeners recompose it through individual and collective engagement.

By understanding listening as composing, Attali aims to overcome the composer-listener divide, which he explains parallels the capitalist producer-worker divide. Rather than serving as a passive consumer, the listener should take agency over their role as coproducer of the musical experience. Stated differently, the agentive listener vibrates with and transforms through musical engagement, avoiding both apathy and the urge for complete control and domination over the experience.

Given Attali's disregard for repetitive music making, he omits the possibility of composing that involves individuals uniquely performing preexisting musical compositions. Yet I think that such understandings follow logically from his work. If a listener can cocompose when listening, then a performer can cocompose through resonant self-expression when performing. As Glenn Gould, a pianist renowned for his interpretations of J. S. Bach's works, once stated, "I believe that the only excuse for being musicians, for making music in any fashion, is to make it differently, and to perform it differently, and to establish the music's difference vis-à-vis our own difference."[19] Gould thus expressed himself by partly recomposing Bach's pieces, and those agentively listening to his performances can do likewise.

The same possibilities hold true for other music practices that may appear repetitive. For instance, while participatory music making often involves highly repetitive musical forms and lines, like the moves within games such as chess, its exact content is "refashioned anew in each performance."[20] Popular musicians may repeat lyrics, phrases, and rhythms, but they typically aim for variations to known songs during live performances. Resonant composing can also involve interpreting tunes that bring one emotional comfort or creating videogame music that personifies one's avatar. The style or form of musical engagement matters less than the self-world relationships that inspire and develop through it. Yet as detailed in chapters 2 and 4, music makers can also enact these processes in ways that reinforce key capitalist values, such as self-promotion and competition. As such, it is important to clarify how resonant composing differs from the relevance-focused music education practices problematized in chapter 2, particularly regarding the role of the teacher.

Resonance relies on deepening qualitative musical distinctions. When educators facilitate students' abilities to go deep into a single musical practice, they enable expression to develop and resonances to vibrate more fully. Such descriptions recall Maxine Greene's assertions about the necessity of sustained, rigorous musical engagement. Offering an example, she writes that Mozart quintets—and, I would add, many forms of music making—do not "reveal all they have to reveal naturally or automatically."[21] While student interests should play a role in resonant composing, too much emphasis on interests, particularly if they alter frequently, can undermine opportunities for extensive, unbroken attention that promotes resonance.

Additionally, surviving the alienation and exploitation inherent in capitalist practices necessitates opportunities for self-love and self-development beyond the identities of consumer, worker, and future worker. Rather than selecting among preformed music choices on an open market, survival-oriented music makers focus on the qualities they bring to and develop through composing. As such, teachers centering resonant composing might consider students' interests alongside concentrated investigation of their cultural histories and local cultural communities. They would focus not only on who the student is, including present wants and interests, but also on who they might become.

Alongside experimenting with one's way of being in the world, resonant composing involves facing fears and insecurities. Like a climber confronting a granite wall or a gymnast approaching a motionless apparatus, the music maker confronts the silent air. Their compositional capacities may mix with hesitation, apprehension, and life baggage as they plunge sound into the void, creating it and themselves anew.

Becoming
I am (not) me
Feeling, moving, relaxing, asserting
Touch emptiness
Hands open, cards displayed
Retract
I win(dow) word(play)
Moments of connecting (that) matter

In addition to experimenting with the aim of resonant composing, music educators and students might explore how various affective flows can counter capitalist alienation. Attali understands composing as a process "to be enjoyed in its own right, its time experienced, rather than labor performed for the sake of using or exchanging its outcome."[22] This description shares similarities with understandings of play, including during musical endeavors.

MUSICAL PLAY

Play is often understood as existing in tension with capitalist work.[23] Vincent Bates explains that through the joyful, freeing, intrinsic motivation central to play, "the bottom line of capitalist production appears to give way."[24] In other words, playful music making emphasizes momentary, often pleasurable experiences and resists capitalist exchanges and ends.

While play cannot be easily defined,[25] play scholar and medical doctor Stuart Brown proposes seven properties of play: "apparently purposeless (done for its own sake), voluntary, inherent attraction, freedom from time, diminished consciousness of self, improvisational potential, and continuation desire."[26] Consider the presence of these properties, which typically resist capitalist ends, in the following hypothetical scenarios:

- Aiming to let off steam from an exhausting chemistry exam and express tenderness felt for a new romantic interest, a high school saxophonist performs the opening melody of John Coltrane's "Giant Steps." Moving into the more technical section of the song, the student laughs at their flailing fingers and inability to keep pace. They then slow down a difficult passage, feeling accomplished after accurately replicating most of the notes. The saxophonist experiments with a few unrelated improvisations and concludes their playing feeling light and energized.

- A five-year-old on a public bus sees an ambulance and breaks into an impromptu song about someone being hurt and needing help, complete with siren sounds. Jolted from their private worries, surrounding passengers chuckle and grin at the child's energy and creativity.

- Individuals of all ages walk amid Pascal Dusapin's *Lullaby Experience*,[27] in which musicians improvise over a piece composed of lullabies from across the world while dancers and attendees levitate on swings and bounce on oversized beds. The curious space creates a sense of peaceful, childlike joy that flows among participants, blurring performer-audience divides.[28]

In these scenarios, each music maker exemplifies Brown's first two properties by engaging voluntarily and without immediate purpose. The high school saxophonist's interpretations and improvisations are their own fleeting end; the musician neither compares their skills to their peers' nor contemplates accolades that might result from their progress. Rather than accumulating an exchangeable value, philosopher Eugen Fink explains, "Play is subject to no end pointing beyond it."[29] The purposes of play reside within play itself.[30]

Additionally, these scenarios exhibit the freedom from time property of play. As bus riders listening to the child's improvisations get lost in the unexpected musical moment, they momentarily forget their worries and to-do lists; they experience a brief reprieve from the normalized acceleration and emotional exhaustion of life under contemporary capitalism. The chuckling riders may also feel the "diminished consciousness of self" aspect of play, in which individuals "stop worrying about whether we look good or awkward, smart or stupid."[31] While those on public transport often avoid eye contact and maintain neutral facial expressions, the child's lifeful song encourages riders to momentarily cease worrying about social norms.

These scenarios also exhibit the property of inherent attraction, which Brown explains as "fun" and making one "feel good."[32] Attendees walking among *Lullaby Experience* likely feel joy while sinking into the oversized beds and serenity on hearing the calming lullabies and accompanying improvisations. As the sustained childlike wonderment encourages ongoing spatial and musical experimentation, participants likely experience the property of continuation desire.[33]

Relatedly, when the participants of *Lullaby Experience* wander among the props, people, and sonic landscape, they might aim to explore, reflect on, and rekindle a sense of curiosity and possibility lost amid capitalist working conditions. Such actions exemplify the improvisational property of play. Brown articulates that during play, "we aren't locked into a rigid way of doing things. We are open to serendipity, to chance. We are willing to include seemingly irrelevant elements into our play."[34] In these respites from work goals and life obligations, participants in all three scenarios probably feel free to imagine. As Fink observes, "In play we enjoy the possibility of retrieving lost possibilities."[35]

Brown's properties of play provide a stark contrast to capitalist alienation. While alienation develops through mandated, clear purposes that resist opportunities for divergent action, play is voluntary, done for its own sake, and has improvisatory potential. Likewise, the inherent attraction, desire for continuation, and freedom from time key to play experiences contrast capitalist working and living conditions, which favor the fleeting thrill of commodity purchasing over meaningful interpersonal engagement. Ongoing commodity accumulation often develops through constantly caring about others' judgment, contrasting playful experiences in which one foregoes worrying about how they appear to fellow participants.

While Brown, like Bates, centers the act of playing, I focus on *playful affects*, meaning the playful sensations that circulate among people and throughout spaces. In this text, I use *play* when referencing activities that typically produce playful affects and *playful affects* when referencing the circulation of sensations emerging from those activities.

PLAYFUL AFFECTIVE FLOWS

As with all affective flows, play necessitates not just specific music practices but particular dispositions and ways of being in the world. Writing about musical play, Roger Mantie observes, "What matters is not so much *what* is done, but *how* it is done."[36] Playful affects emerge as much from individual and collective approaches to activities as from the design of a specific musical activity.

Playful affects move among spaces and people without a clear destination or end point. Such circulation mirrors Alan Watts's observations about playfulness and dance. He explains, "You don't aim at a particular spot in the room because that's where you will arrive. The whole point of dancing is the dance."[37] Likewise, playful affects bounce vibrantly among individuals and groups, creating atmospheres of possibility.

Playful affects w

a

n

d
e
r
ful(l) of un
expected
POP and wonder
Dancing in irc
c l
se
s . s
q e and sh p
u a r a es that de
f
y
a
l bel
s
They smile and on occasion frown, but
never accumulate, dictate, or irritate
Imagined meshings of
child's babbling
Inter-stitched sunbeams
Weightless daydream

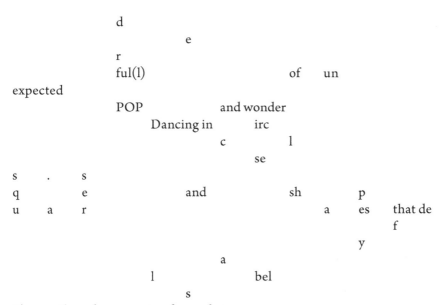

REFUESE, they must, the confines of work:😛

Playful affective flows that fluctuate without propagating outward provide an alternative to expanding affective flows that parallel ongoing capitalist growth. The imagined five-year-old child does not aim to compose a song they can perform or even repeat a second time. Engrossed fully in each fleeting note, the child seeks neither affirmation nor a response from listeners, enabling playful affects to circulate rather than accumulate. However, should the child's parent enroll them in a singing competition or use their musicality to advocate for admittance into an elite kindergarten, then the expressive, playful affective flows transform into expansive, capitalistic ones.

Importantly, playful affective flows can involve diverse emotions and feelings. Participants in the three aforementioned music endeavors may experience emotions ranging from contentment to nervousness to delight, and their individual feelings interface with and inform affective flows among participants. Demanding the presence of joy or other feelings can undermine the spontaneity and uncertainty inherent in play. As Sara Ahmed explains, when happiness—or, I would add, any emotion or feeling—becomes its own end, endeavors become useful in forwarding those affects, thus limiting potential improvisations.[38] Stated differently, music education practices that aim for specific affective ends inhibit both other emergent qualities and possible trajectories of playful affects. Yet this does not mean that playful affects are incompatible with all specified aims.

If judgments neither become ends in themselves nor overtake one's enjoyment or desire to continue the endeavor, then playful affective flows can coexist alongside distinctions and evaluations. Although completely standardized goals lack the openness to possibilities characteristic of play, playful affects can circulate among improvisatory musical games, amateur songwriting contests, or even semistandardized forms of competition. One can feel frustrated while perfecting an improvisation or disappointed that they did not live up to their own standards at a public performance while still approaching such endeavors playfully. However, the more others impose immutable standards on students, the less likely playful affects will emerge.

Combining the overarching aim of resonant composing with practices fostering the emergence and circulation of playful affects can contribute to more robust and meaningful survival under capitalism. Resonant composing and playful affective flows, however, can still reinforce capitalist ills.

LIMITS OF RESONANT COMPOSING AND PLAYFUL AFFECTIVE FLOWS

While the aim of resonant composing and the circulation of playful affects provide alternatives to capitalist alienation, they may contribute to other problematic aspects of capitalism, thus undermining more robust survival opportunities. Composing and play can serve self-branding and other forms of competition, encourage unrestrained consumption and accumulation, and facilitate the development of new commodities that others purchase. I address each of these three points of alignment in turn.

Exchanged for Self-Branding

First, both resonant composing and play can promote self-branding and other capitalist uses. Marx distinguishes between a commodity's use value and its exchange value. Use value refers to a commodity's ability to serve a specific human's need or want.[39] For example, water has a high use value to all individuals. Alternatively, an original Beethoven score may have a high use value to a musicologist specializing in nineteenth-century Europe but a low use value to an Australian jazz guitarist. Often expressed through money, exchange value develops through the trading of use values. The price a Beethoven score can bring at auction constitutes its exchange value.

Use value and exchange value are not necessarily correlated. For example, an old guitar may have a high use value to a student without access to other musical instruments but would likely have a low exchange value. However, capitalist economic practices encourage individuals to link use value and exchange value. Music software enabling more nuanced sound manipulation will not necessarily have higher use value for average consumers than more basic software, but its producers will aim to ensure it possesses a higher exchange value. This higher exchange value encourages consumers to assume that it has higher use value for them. The linking of use and exchange values may cause consumers to spend more for commodities with features unnecessary for their purposes.

Exchange value may take forms other than money, particularly in music education. Joseph Abramo explains judges' scores at music competitions as a representation of the exchange value of a musical performance.[40] While such performances may involve personally fulfilling composing, when students and teachers exchange labor for a numeric score from a judge, their playful music making has the potential for use as self-promotion. Parents could encourage the imagined playful jazz saxophone student to engage in competitions and use accolades to increase chances of entrance at elite colleges. Given that standardization limits the improvisatory aspect of play, the exchange value of scores will likely overtake the use value of play.

Likewise, when play supports self-aggrandizement, the use value of personal growth can transform into self-branding, which has the potential to enhance the exchange value of one's future endeavors. For instance, imagine attendees at *Lullaby Experience* posting selfies that further their personal brands as modern artistic individuals. Although attendees may initially experience purposelessness, freedom from time, diminished consciousness of self, and other properties of play, their attention-seeking social media posts transform those moments into self-serving and competitive practices that can contribute to enhanced compensation for one's work.

Similarly, while educators and students might experience playful resonance during a specific musical engagement, bragging about their accomplishments on social media may enhance their social positionality. No longer a private joy, the shared musical accomplishment becomes an opportunity to enhance standing and influence among peers and within professional networks. This new positionality may enable them to demand an increased exchange value for their labor. It may also lead to more prestigious work, education, and leisure opportunities; through such processes, individual advancement overtakes playful experiences.

Furthermore, many resonant, playful music education performance events function as capitalist exchanges. Even absent admission charges, audience members often understand concerts as repayment for the time and energy they have invested in students' music education. The audience receives and accumulates what the students produce.

Repeated uses, including their resulting exchange values, inform and limit the nature of activities. As Ahmed explains, "A history of use is a history of becoming natural."[41] When repeatedly used for exchangeable ends, like recognition and self-promotion, music education can surpass any personal use values students and teachers initially bring to such endeavors. Over time, using music education to enhance one's self-brand and worker identity becomes normalized and unquestioned. Such action benefits capitalist producers by enhancing worker competition and opportunities for exploitation while furthering teachers' and students' alienation.

Unrestrained Consumption

In addition to self-branding and competition, a second way capitalist producers extract profit from both resonant composing and musical play is by encouraging unrestrained consumption and accumulation. Regardless of aims or affects, music creating, performing, and listening can stimulate the purchasing of more and more software, instruments, recordings, and music services, primarily benefiting capitalist producers. Those seeking to continually refine their playful composing capacities may unthinkingly purchase an ever-changing array of commodities, ranging from the latest DJing software to historical items to custom-made instruments. In the process, capitalist producers extract profit from each purchase.

Moreover, Brown explains that when individuals feel unable to control the attraction, freedom from time, and continuation desire aspects of playful experiences, they can turn playful affects emerging from video gaming, gambling, or other endeavors into addictions that lead to unrestrained spending and consumption, not to mention other ills.[42] The music maker unable to control their playful attraction to composing with GarageBand or Ableton Live may invest significant money into purchasing new loops, digital instruments, and other software add-ons and updates. In addition to potentially furthering alienation by isolating the composer from face-to-face interactions, such action benefits the capitalist producers who make and sell the software. Likewise, musicians working in genres ranging from classical to popular to avant-garde can become obsessed with purchasing music recordings and new instruments as well as technology ranging from apps to amplifiers to recording devices. While it is hard to imagine playful composing absent any resources, the ongoing attraction key to such practices can encourage the unending desire for more and better products, furthering capitalist consumption and accumulation while increasing profits for capitalist producers.

The same holds true for playful music education opportunities. Within almost all music genres, individuals can pay exorbitant prices for elite lessons or interactive events with their favorite music makers. They can spend significant sums of money on online music courses or other instructional materials and memberships. While some of this profit goes to skilled music teachers, who are members of the working class rather than the capitalist class, members of wealthy publishing and events companies likely also benefit from these exchanges. Those seeking playful musical composing in order to survive capitalism may therefore end up enhancing capitalist producers' wealth, furthering their own and others' economic entrenchment. Stated differently, when unrestrained consumption of musical goods that promote playful composing becomes the solution to capitalist alienation, music makers undermine their own survival.

Play itself can also be marketed to consumers. While the Institut de Recherche et Coordination Acoustique/Musique made *Lullaby Experience* freely available to French citizens, capitalist producers may charge exclusionary admission fees to similar playful musical events. For example, consider the five million people who paid up to $59.90 to attend an immersive Van Gogh experience in which visitors see the painter's images through a combination of virtual reality and humongous, 360-degree motion-filled screens.[43] In alignment with capitalist ideals of self-aggrandizement and competition, the website home page brags that the exhibit was "awarded best 2021 immersive experience by *USA Today*" and "ranked among the 12 best immersive experiences in the world by CNN."[44] Regardless of whether attendees use the exhibit as a form of self-promotion, their playful art making enhances capitalist producers' profits. Although environmentally conscious artistic consumption is not in and of itself problematic, consumption within capitalist systems necessarily benefits capitalist producers.

Commodity Creation

Third, both resonant composing and playful affective flows can enable the formation of new commodities that spur consumption. Even if individuals undertake playful endeavors without a clear aim, improvisational potential can lead to inventions and innovations that they or others may develop. Consider a playful music composition endeavor that a student posts on YouTube or TikTok absent any compensation. Such music making furthers other viewers' insatiable music consumption, creating added profits for behemoth companies. While the video poster may experience a sense of survival through playful composing, they have contributed to ever-growing capitalist expansion. They have also allowed capitalist companies to profit from free labor, thus disincentivizing them from adequately compensating professional musicians whose livelihoods depend on such exchanges.

In short, both the aim of resonant composing and the circulation of playful affects may support capitalist ends, including self-aggrandizement, ongoing accumulation, and creative innovations that others consume. Useless music making might provide an alternative to such action. Ahmed explains that to be useless "is not to support what is being accomplished."[45] In Marx's terms, useless music making would not have an exchange value and would therefore avoid creating profit for capitalist producers. It follows that survival-focused music educators and students might engage in music making useless to capitalist producers.

BECOMING USELESS THROUGH TRACELESS MUSICAL GIFTS

Being useless to capitalism can involve avoiding, as much as possible, the purchasing of music-related commodities. Teachers and students might create instruments from trash or unused materials or sew uniforms from old clothing. Working with woodshop teachers or other school or community personnel, they could use free materials to create instruments for themselves or others. In addition to not benefiting capitalist producers, such action shows students that they can engage in survival-focused musical endeavors regardless of their economic positionality.

Importantly, cheap products do not necessarily generate less profit for capitalist producers. Through planned obsolescence, in which nondurable materials, changed designs, and unavailable spare parts encourage constant replacement of commodities, cheap products can further consumption. As such, thoughtfully designed, long-lasting music resources may benefit capitalist producers less than disposable commodities that quickly become obsolete.

Furthermore, when music makers must purchase commodities, they might question who benefits from their purchases. This reflection involves considering the working conditions under which commodities are produced as well as how companies selling music products distribute their profits. Whenever possible, music educators and students might favor companies that promote environmental resource sustainability and treat workers humanely, including through equitable distribution of profits to all employees. Importantly, teachers can involve students and parents in discussions about who they are purchasing certain products from and why. Considerations about music purchases alone, however, will not stop playful composing from reinforcing the aforementioned capitalist ills associated with self-branding and unconsidered commodity creation.

Traceless Music Making

In order for music making to enhance self-aggrandizement or inspire commodities others can consume, it must leave a trace. Traces involve the capturing and reproducing of music making or its byproducts, such as judges' scores or innovative thinking. Examples of musical traces include recordings, social media posts, and creative ideas that enable new products.

Conversely, consider the "leave no trace" ethic promoted to preserve wilderness areas from destruction by recreational users. While the exact origins of leave no trace are unknown, versions of this idea began circulating among United States conservationists in the mid-twentieth century and were codified in the 1980s.[46] The basic goal of the leave no trace ethic is that individuals enjoy wilderness areas while impacting them as minimally as possible. For example, the presence of trash and needless off-trail trampling of vegetation diminish other visitors' enjoyment of wilderness scenery. Leaving few, if any, traces of one's visit enables more visitors to experience pristine wilderness while sustaining and protecting natural ecologies.

Applying a similar ethic to music education, traceless music making involves not leaving anything from which capitalist producers, including individual entrepreneurial participants, might benefit. If music making leaves no trace, then producers cannot retain it, and it is therefore useless in terms of producing a profit. Such action mirrors Attali's imagining of music making that "is no longer made to be represented or stockpiled, but for participation in collective play. . . . It becomes nonreproducible, irreversible."[47]

More specifically, consider two leave no trace principles: "Pack out everything brought into the wilderness" and "Properly dispose of anything that can't be packed out."[48] Adapting these ideas to music education might involve class periods, concerts, or other endeavors at which participants agree not to retain evidence of the event, including recordings or social media posts. Such action resists both participants and observers using survival-focused music making to encourage self-branding and consumption. However, since participants may want to retain traces of musical events for reasons that have little to do with self-promotion, such as private sharing with a family member unable to attend in person, music educators and students might consider when and why to embrace traceless music making.

Importantly, Ahmed distinguishes between *unused* and *useless*. Unused resources are passive and thus waiting to be used.[49] As such, unused class time is devoid of thoughtful musical actions and aims. Deeming something *unused* can help justify its appropriation.[50] For example, United States companies have appropriated dormant natural resources in Latin America and elsewhere by declaring that using these unused resources have both local and global benefits. Likewise, if school administrators come to understand music class time as unused, they might appropriate that time for math, science, or other subjects they deem useful within contemporary capitalist economies. Even if administrators do not to appropriate unused class time, since passive, completely aimless teaching undermines opportunities for resonant composing, it does not contribute to students' survival.

In contrast, that which is useless, including traceless, is active and evolving. Ahmed explains that objects, people, and practices deemed *useless* directly resist appropriation for capitalist ends.[51] Traceless music making involves concerted attention to how individuals and corporations could co-opt it for capitalist uses, followed by steps to resist and undermine such practices. A useless music class is vibrant and eventful, just not in ways that enhance students' or others' entrepreneurial selves. For example, a traceless music class might set up private online spaces in which students collaboratively decide who should access their recordings and other creations. Focusing solely on traceless music making, however, can negate opportunities to enhance others' survival through sharing artistic endeavors beyond one's immediate community.

Musical Gift Giving

Survival-focused teachers and students wishing to engage broader communities might reconceive of their playful compositions as what essayist Lewis Hyde explains as gifts.[52] Since gift exchanges occur without money, they create neither surplus value nor profit and are thus useless for capitalism. As professor and member of the Citizen Potawatomi Nation Robin Wall Kimmerer explains, "A gift is different from something you buy, possessed of meaning outside its material boundaries. You never dishonor the gift. A gift asks something of you. To take care of it. And something more."[53]

Unlike a purchased commodity, which remains in the purchaser's possession, Hyde draws on the gift-giving practices of various Indigenous peoples to explain that received gifts are given away in turn rather than kept.[54] In other words, gifts remain in continual motion; a gift that cannot be given away is no longer a gift.[55] Kimmerer elaborates: "We are bound in a covenant of reciprocity, a pact of mutual responsibility to sustain those who sustain us."[56] While not completely traceless, gift giving resists capitalist accumulation, since one cannot amass what they must give away.

Imagine a gift-focused musical exchange in which participants have no expectation of experiencing music making. This might involve sharing music in places where people do not expect it, ranging from school offices to public parks to community centers. Gift-focused music making might involve populations of people, including children and adults uninterested in sitting quietly at a concert, who do not expect the school or community group to make music in ways they could enjoy and thus receive as a gift. However, since the gift giver initiates the process, such action contrasts situations in which music makers are asked to provide labor for free at specific events.

Just as gift givers select gifts they anticipate receivers will find meaningful, gift-focused music makers would adjust their practices for intended receiver-participants. This might involve songs written for or dedicated to certain individuals or groups or interactive exchanges involving dancing, singing, or drumming. As Kimmerer explains, "Often, if the giveaway is small and personal, every gift will be handmade. Sometimes a whole community might work all year long to fashion the presents for guests they do not even know."[57]

Since gifts individuals find meaningful often fulfill wishes or interests at least partially hidden to the receiver, they typically involve an aspect of surprise. As such, facilitators of gift-oriented music events might consider the types of music participants would find meaningful but not necessarily seek out on their own. Such action differs from relevant music making, which is usually synonymous with the capitalist aim of capturing and holding participants' attention.[58]

The circulation of gifts tends to establish relationships between givers and receivers.[59] Students and audience-participants who experience musical events as gifts would feel a sense of obligation to reciprocate. Ideally, these receivers would then circulate their own gifts, musical or otherwise, with others.

A key part of this reciprocal relationship is gratitude. Through a sense of gratitude for the gift, the receiver feels an unpaid debt that motivates how they reciprocate.[60] Kimmerer elaborates: "In a culture of gratitude, everyone knows that gifts will follow the circle of reciprocity and flow back to you again. . . . The grass in the ring is trodden down in a path from gratitude to reciprocity. We dance in a circle, not in a line."[61] This gratitude contrasts the impersonal, alienating relationship between capitalist producers and consumers, in which one may feel entitled to music making absent any responsibility to music makers.

Hyde understands return gifts as the ultimate act of gratitude, and thus "the true acceptance of the original gift."[62] Yet he clarifies that the initial receiver determines what constitutes a countergift, and a return gift cannot be an explicit condition of the initial exchange.[63] Gift receivers should therefore not feel a worrisome sense of obligation to return the gift; return gift giving is an unprompted, intrinsically motivated endeavor. Additionally, as exemplified by Kimmerer's image of a circle, gifts often move onward to other individuals rather than directly back to the initial giver. A gift exchange therefore differs significantly from a quid pro quo arrangement, in which a return favor is expected, if not demanded. Gift-based music experiences invite and welcome participants while acknowledging that gifts may go unaccepted.

Hyde posits that through the experience of gratitude, a gift can change the receiver.[64] How receivers grow in and through the gift-giving process determines the nature of reciprocation. Wandering possibilities and personal growth inform the playful gift-giving process. For this reason, a receiver cannot determine the nature of the return gift in advance.

Additionally, understanding artistic endeavors as gifts rather than commodities can open opportunities for more authentic personal expression. In an extensive study of blood-giving practices in various countries, Richard Titmuss found that individuals who donated blood voluntarily—providing it as a gift—were more likely than individuals who received compensation for their blood to answer truthfully a questionnaire addressing potential risky behaviors (e.g., drug use) that could contaminate their blood.[65] Titmuss argues that in thinking primarily about how payment could enhance their own opportunities in a market economy, those compensated for their blood centered their freedom and not the freedom of others who may experience harm because of contaminated blood.[66]

A similar parallel may exist in terms of personal and collective composing. When individuals receive payment or other forms of compensation, like grades, for their music making, they cannot help but let the judgment of audiences, evaluators, and other stakeholders influence their composing. Conversely, when music makers understand their work as a gift, they have more freedom to express their authentic, constantly developing selves. Although meaningful gift giving necessitates considering the impact of one's composing on others, gift-focused music makers can express themselves more truthfully and playfully because they do not suffer economic consequences from their decisions.

Importantly, gift giving is distinct from charity. Hyde argues that gift giving can occur only within each social class.[67] If a person in a high socioeconomic class gives a gift to a person in a low socioeconomic class, the latter may not necessarily reciprocate the exchange in a way that the former finds meaningful and transformative, or vice versa. Furthermore, absent economic equity among participants, gift giving can advance the problematic capitalist narrative that individuals exploited by capitalist practices should accept and show gratitude to those doing the exploitation.

While I address how music educators and students might challenge material inequities in chapter 7, survival-focused gift giving necessarily occurs among members of the same social class. Although such action undermines opportunities for interclass understanding, the circulation of musical gifts among the working class may promote a sense of collaborative community that can contribute to the political action needed to address capitalist inequities.[68] Additionally, I acknowledge that drawing on Indigenous knowledge to offer an alternative to capitalist practices could be interpreted as an act of colonization. In order to address this problematic appropriation of thinking from historically and currently exploited communities, music educators might, whenever possible, pair gift-giving music education practices with the resisting and challenging practices described in chapter 6 and 7.

More broadly, understanding music making as a gift rather than a capitalist transaction can encourage those who love music making to seek other careers while still practicing their art. Hyde explains that such action enables marketplace wealth to be converted into gift wealth, since art makers would transform the money earned through working capitalist jobs into resources supporting their artistic gift giving.[69] Part of surviving capitalism might therefore involve intentionally separating capitalist work from gift-giving musical endeavors, as well as devoting significant time and resources to the latter.

MORE EQUITABLE SURVIVING

Thus far, I have argued that surviving capitalist exploitation might involve resonant composing and playful affective flows. To avoid the potential for such music making to serve capitalist ends, music educators and students might consider the traceless nature of their playful composing. They might also create playful compositions that circulate as gifts others find meaningful. Yet students already marginalized through exploitative capitalist practices may experience these processes differently than those facing less exploitation. The practices discussed in this chapter will not directly alter capitalist material inequities, but music teachers and students can focus on enhancing the survival of those experiencing the greatest financial need. Although decisions about enhanced survival should always be made with substantial input from students and local communities, I offer four potential starting considerations.

First, music educators might consider redistributing available time and material resources needed for playful composing to students with the fewest financial resources. Within elementary music education classes or other universal music education programs, teachers might ask which forms of playful musical composing students from lower socioeconomic status backgrounds find most meaningful. Within elective music education programs, teachers might focus on creating playful classes that attract and retain students from lower socioeconomic class backgrounds. Teachers would then prioritize budgets and voluntary before- or after-school time to support such learning. Importantly, endeavors would focus on qualitative distinctions that extend and develop students' expressivity rather than defaulting to relevant music making that captures and holds students' attention.

A second related consideration is that resonant composing necessarily involves locally constructed and historically connected self-knowledge. Foregrounding the histories and compositional interests of students facing the greatest material inequities can empower them to express themselves more vibrantly and authentically. Imagining a social justice curriculum for the elementary classroom, Bree Picower explains that "when students are supported to learn more about their own history, they are better able to identify, deconstruct, and not internalize harmful stereotypes about their identities."[70] Since students privileged by ability, class, race, and other qualities often learn idealized group histories and develop much self-knowledge throughout their schooling, more equitable surviving would involve teachers inverting those priorities and relationships.

Focusing on the histories and expressive desires of students facing material inequities differs from diversity initiatives focused solely on recognition. Instead of only recognizing the histories of transgender, differently abled, or Black, Brown, Indigenous, and Asian students, such histories would center the past and present laws, institutions, and practices that undermine the economic flourishing of such individuals. Music educators would also attend to the histories, exploitations, and compositional needs of low socioeconomic class white students. Centering local knowledge will likely necessitate foregoing or minimizing certain music standards as well as extending or finding alternatives to existing resources and curricula.

Third, since individuals excluded from material flourishing cannot necessarily express themselves within dominant forms of music making, more equitable playful composing might involve openness to experimentation with music practices that defy genre boundaries. For example, Attali explains that since free jazz involved the meshing of Black popular music with "more abstract theoretical explorations of European music," such practices "created *locally* the conditions for a different model of musical production" that refused existing musical hierarchies.[71] When music educators encourage students to expand their playful composing beyond existing genres and confines, they challenge capitalist categorizations and hierarchies, such as the placing of popular or country music as superior to rap and hip-hop. By considering how educators and students might make creations traceless, they resist their work serving as commodities from which capitalist producers could profit.

Fourth, promoting more equitable surviving via musical gifts means examining who receives those gifts and whether they find them meaningful. Picower explains that providing students opportunities to learn about and appreciate their local environments enables them "to operate from a place of pride about their communities rather than fall victim to messages that claim that their communities are the cause of their problems."[72] Likewise, playful musical gift giving within and among communities deprived of material equity stems from and may develop pride within those communities.

Music educators and policymakers may worry that foregrounding playful composing will further marginalize music education within schools and communities. Yet as Bates argues, "The price of their capitulation to neoliberal rationalities is that, by reifying those rationalities for the sake of self-preservation, music education runs the real risk of 'selling its soul' by suppressing rather than amplifying the personally fulfilling potential of musical play."[73] Extending Bates, I offer that if music educators do not consider what experiences best enable students to survive within contemporary inequitable, alienating capitalist practices, they predestine most students to fail in a system designed only to serve an elite few. Moreover, if capitalism remains for the foreseeable future, one of the best ways to challenge it may be momentarily living out alternatives to it. I invite you to play with that useless thought. 😃

In the spirit of *Choose Your Own Adventure* books, continue onto chapter 6 for an examination of resisting capitalist inequities. Alternatively, for an investigation of how music educators and students might directly challenge capitalist inequities, skip to chapter 7. To consider more equitable thriving within capitalism, turn to chapter 4.

NOTES

1. According to researchers at the National Center for Education Statistics, "a smaller percentage of students of low socioeconomic status (SES) than students of middle SES attained a bachelor's or higher degree within 8 years of high school completion (14 vs. 29 percent), and percentages for both groups were smaller than the percentage of high-SES students who attained this level of education (60 percent)." "Postsecondary Attainment: Differences by Socioeconomic Status," *National Center for Education Statistics*, 2015, https://nces.ed.gov/programs/coe/pdf/coe_tva.pdf.

2. "Global Wealth Report 2021," *Credit Suisse*, June 2021, https://www.credit-suisse.com/about-us/en/reports-research/global-wealth-report.html.

3. Karl Marx, *Economic and Philosophic Manuscripts of 1844*, trans. Martin Milligan (Amherst, NY: Prometheus Books, 1988), 69–84.

4. Michel Foucault, *Discipline and Punish: The Birth of the Prison*, trans. Alan Sheridan (New York: Vintage Books, 1995), 135–65.

5. Cathy Benedict, "Processes of Alienation: Marx, Orff and Kodaly," *British Journal of Music Education* 26, no. 2 (2009): 213–24. While not grounded in Marx's philosophy, Thomas Regelski makes a similar critique of music education methods. See Thomas Regelski, "On 'Methodolatry' and Music Teaching as Critical and Reflective Praxis," *Philosophy of Music Education Review* 10, no. 2 (2002): 102–23.

6. Jacques Attali, *Noise: The Political Economy of Music*, trans. Brian Massumi (Minneapolis: University of Minnesota Press, 1985), 87–132.

7. See, for example, Lydia Goehr, *The Imaginary Museum of Musical Works: An Essay in the Philosophy of Music* (New York: Oxford University Press, 2007).

8. Attali, *Noise*, 87–132.

9. Attali, *Noise*, 133–48.

10. Attali, *Noise*, 133–48.

11. Attali, *Noise*, 134.

12. Attali, *Noise*, 143.

13. I am grateful to Cara Bernard for proposing this example.

14. Hartmut Rosa, *Resonance: A Sociology of Our Relationship to the World*, trans. James C. Wagner (Cambridge: Polity Press, 2019). For a detailed explanation of resonance, see chapter 3.

15. Attali, *Noise*, 133–43.

16. Rosa, *Resonance*, 184.

17. State Education Agency Directors of Arts Education, "National Core Arts Standards," 2014, http://nationalartsstandards.org/.

18. Attali, *Noise*, 135.

19. *Genius Within: The Inner Life of Glenn Gould*, directed by Michèle Hozer and Peter Raymont (White Pine Pictures, 2009).

20. Thomas Turino, *Music as Social Life: The Politics of Participation* (Chicago: University of Chicago Press, 2008), 59.
21. Maxine Greene, *Variations on a Blue Guitar: The Lincoln Center Institute Lectures on Aesthetic Education* (New York: Teachers College Press, 2001), 20.
22. Attali, *Noise*, 142.
23. See, for example, Vincent Bates, "Music Education, Neoliberal Social Reproduction, and Play," *Action, Criticism, and Theory for Music Education* 20, no. 3 (2021): 92–93; Roger Mantie, *Music, Leisure, Education: Historical and Philosophical Perspectives* (New York: Oxford University Press, 2022), 170–6.
24. Bates, "Music Education," 97.
25. Stuart Brown, *Play: How It Shapes the Brain, Opens the Imagination, and Invigorates the Soul* (New York: Penguin Group, 2009), X.
26. Brown, *Play*, 24–25.
27. See Pascal Dusapin, *Lullaby Experience*, https://www.youtube.com/watch?v=aFqFlOZmYls.
28. I am grateful to Alex Tedrow for bringing this example to my attention.
29. Eugen Fink, *Play as Symbol of the World*, trans. Ian Alexander Moore and Christopher Turner (Bloomington: Indiana University Press, 2016), 213.
30. Fink, *Play as Symbol of the World*, 209.
31. Brown, *Play*, 25.
32. Brown, *Play*, 25.
33. Brown, *Play*, 25.
34. Brown, *Play*, 17.
35. Fink, *Play as Symbol of the World*, 90.
36. Mantie, *Music, Leisure, Education*, 170.
37. Alan Watts, "You Play the Piano," accessed August 27, 2022, https://www.awakin.org/v2/read/view.php?tid=2212.
38. Sara Ahmed, *What's the Use?* (Durham, NC: Duke University Press, 2019), 127.
39. Karl Marx, *Capital: A Critique of Political Economy, Volume One*, trans. Ben Fowkes (New York: Penguin Books, 2004), 126.
40. Joseph Abramo, "The Phantasmagoria of Competition in School Ensembles," *Philosophy of Music Education Review* 23, no. 2 (2017): 150–70.
41. Ahmed, *What's the Use?* 41.
42. Brown, *Play*, 172–89.
43. I am grateful to Cara Bernard for suggesting this example.
44. Van Gogh: The Immersive Experience, https://vangoghexpo.com.
45. Ahmed, *What's the Use?* 104.
46. David N. Cole, "Leave No Trace: How It Came to Be," *International Journal of Wilderness* 24, no. 3 (2018): 54–65.
47. Attali, *Noise*, 141.
48. Cole, "Leave No Trace," 58.
49. Ahmed, *What's the Use?* 48.

50. Ahmed, *What's the Use?* 48.

51. Ahmed, *What's the Use?* 48.

52. Lewis Hyde, *The Gift: Creativity and the Artist in the Modern World* (New York: Vintage Books, 2007), 4.

53. Robin Wall Kimmerer, *Braiding Sweetgrass: Indigenous Wisdom, Scientific Knowledge and the Teachings of Plants* (Minneapolis, MN: Milkweed Editions, 2013), 382.

54. Hyde, *Gift*, 4.

55. Hyde, *Gift*, xix.

56. Kimmerer, *Braiding Sweetgrass*, 382.

57. Kimmerer, *Braiding Sweetgrass*, 381.

58. For further discussion of the relationship between relevance and capitalism, see chapter 2.

59. Hyde, *Gift*, xx.

60. Hyde, *Gift*, 65.

61. Kimmerer, *Braiding Sweetgrass*, 381.

62. Hyde, *Gift*, 65.

63. Hyde, *Gift*, 11.

64. Hyde, *Gift*, 65.

65. Richard M. Titmuss, *The Gift Relationship: From Human Blood to Social Policy* (New York: New Press, 1997).

66. Titmuss, *Gift Relationship*, 308.

67. Hyde, *Gift*, 180.

68. In chapter 6, I further address this idea of collaborative resistance.

69. Hyde, *Gift*, 359.

70. Bree Picower, "Using Their Words: Six Elements of Social Justice Curriculum Design for the Elementary Classroom," *International Journal of Multicultural Education* 14, no. 1 (2012): 5.

71. Attali, *Noise*, 140.

72. Picower, "Using Their Words," 5.

73. Bates, "Music Education," 98.

SIX

RESISTING CAPITALIST MATERIAL INEQUITIES THROUGH DIALOGIC WITNESSING

IN ADDITION TO THE POSSIBILITIES of thriving within and surviving under capitalism, music teachers and students might consider how they could address capitalist ills. As argued throughout this text, the material inequities key to capitalist systems propagate in part because individuals come to understand the values and dispositions that support them as natural and unquestionable. Music educators and students may have trouble imagining their work apart from competitions and self-branding that reinforce the accumulation, self-centeredness, and entrepreneurship key to capitalism. If music educators find capitalism-related ills—including material inequities detailed in chapter 1—problematic, then they might consider their potential role in resisting them.

I offer that resisting capitalist material inequities involves facilitating students' development of skills and dispositions important for sustained, equity-focused cooperative engagements within current socioeconomic systems. The pyramidal structure of capitalism means that working-class individuals far outnumber politically influential capitalist-class stakeholders and groups. Silvia Federici argues that it is "where communal bonds are the strongest that capitalism is halted and even forced to recede."[1] When enough people affected by capitalism-related problems come together to address these issues, they have the potential to gain concessions from members of the capitalist class.

Resisting involves both raising students' awareness about capitalist inequities and providing them with the practices needed to work collaboratively with diverse stakeholders throughout their lives. Understanding resisting as a lifelong process necessitates the conviction that cooperation among those in the middle and bottom of capitalist pyramidal structures can improve their socioeconomic circumstances. As opposed to provoking direct responses to capitalist inequities, which I address in the challenging capitalism chapter, resisting emphasizes more long-term socioeconomic changes. Resisting aims for the transfer of understandings to future endeavors; it requires patient persistence in the absence of immediate progress toward material equity. Before proposing music education practices that might contribute to the skills and dispositions needed to resist capitalist inequities, I consider how pervasive contemporary music education practices may inhibit the development of such skills and dispositions.

LIMITS OF MUSIC COLLABORATION AND LISTENING

At first glance, teachers might think that the collaboration key for resisting capitalist ills already develops in their classrooms. Indeed, music education practices, ranging from elementary student group singing to steel pan and Mariachi ensembles, have the potential to unite diverse individuals in a single purpose. While the communal nature of such endeavors differs from the more individualistic achievement focus of K-12 classes such as math and science, musical collaboration is often a straightforward, uncontested transaction.

Taking direction from an authoritative leader, as typically occurs in group music-making settings, differs from the messiness typically needed for political action. For example, while popular leaders such as Martin Luther King Jr. attracted and galvanized large groups of people, the civil rights movement ultimately relied on layers of collaborative organizing in which individuals creatively navigated tensions to reach coconstructed goals. Such scenarios differ from top-down music education models, in which students typically listen to various musical voices with the intent of matching and assimilating. Although conductorless Western art music making could serve as a model for collaborative civic interactions, in much current general and ensemble music education, conformity and replication take precedence over communal negotiation of different, sometimes competing perspectives.

Alternatively, popular music making often revolves around individual icons and narratives about personally conquering adversity. Musicologist William Cheng explains that music reality competitions, such as *American Idol* and *The Voice*, play up narratives of individuals overcoming challenging circumstances, including forms of disability. He observes, "But insofar as reality competitions cash in on these token appearances by contestants with impairments, the format may end up treating adversity in exploitative, reductive ways. Disability, neatly packaged, enables producers to turn stories of plight into profit."[2] In addition to financially benefiting media conglomerates, these popular music narratives forward the inaccurate idea that with a little effort, all people can easily overcome the circumstances of their birth, including minimal material resources and social support.

Placing the burden of financial success on individual music makers minimizes attention to how capitalist pyramidal structures by definition inhibit most people from financial thriving. Individual narratives may even afford viewers "a fantasy of community, an opportunity to feel together—crying and emoting and being overcome along with contestants, judges, studio audience members, and other fans watching across the nation."[3] In such moments, community becomes synonymous with supporting another individual's popularity and accompanying financial gain. Such conceptions of success and community can make collaborative resisting of capitalist ills appear unnecessary, promoting individualism that undermines the communal negotiations needed within the working class to resist capitalist inequities.

One might argue that listening to another's musical expression can serve as a starting place for the complicated collaborations with diverse stakeholders necessary for resisting material inequities. I agree that cooperation necessitates actively listening to different voices. However, such listening does not necessarily occur through engagement with televised music competitions or typical music classes.

Few music educators would allow one student to rudely interrupt or talk over another, and they typically expect students to remain quiet during live and recorded music making. However, these practices can occur without any listening. A student who does not interrupt others or remains quiet during others' music making is certainly compliant, but they are not necessarily internalizing the sounds around them. Even when a teacher requests that students demonstrate their listening by, for example, keeping a steady beat or making an observation about a performance, students may only provide the minimum attention necessary to respond. One could, for instance, hear Billie Holiday's rhythmic nuances and vocal inflections but not the narrative and cultural connections expressed through her singing.

Students can also listen without honoring what they hear. A student may comprehend musical and contextual aspects of a performance but not respect its creators or performers. For example, they might take the music making of a transgender woman less seriously than that of a cisgender man. As Cheng notes, the world does not lack people motivated to find, create, and appreciate beauty: "What's actually in short supply—what lies at the root of so much injury and injustice—is people's limited capacity or willingness to understand, tolerate, and dignify the different things that *other people* find beautiful."[4] If listening is a necessary but insufficient disposition for collaboration that could resist capitalist inequities, then what other music education practices might contribute to such efforts?

DIALOGIC AFFECTIVE FLOWS

Dialogue plays a key role in the formation and enactment of collaborations that can resist and ultimately challenge inequitable capitalist distribution practices. As Maxine Greene notes, spaces in which there exist "dialogue and exchanges of all kinds" foster the groundwork for a "public empowered and encouraged to speak for itself, perhaps in many voices."[5] While one might initially conceive of dialogue as a primarily cognitive endeavor, all dialogue involves emotional aspects, as emotion and cognition exist inseparably.[6]

Favoring cognitive aspects of dialogue over emotional ones can encourage incomplete or inaccurate communication. For example, one might not ponder why anger underpins certain words in a song or how the emotional tone of an instrumental solo implies meanings counter to those typically associated with similar musical phrases. Alternatively, centering the affective aspect of artistic dialogues can highlight how emotions inform meaning making and contribute to shared understandings. Examining why a student chose to express sadness in a certain part of their composition enables peers and teachers to respond more thoughtfully, perhaps by taking action in solidarity with the student.

Dialogic affective flows involve continual back-and-forth exchanges. Like all affective flows, dialogic affective flows continually fluctuate as they move among and beyond individuals, at times temporarily cohering as feelings within individuals. In dialogic affective flows, parties build off, from, and with each other.

Beginning from a place of dignity and respect, those engaged in dialogic affective flows avoid making assumptions or prejudgments about the value of others' music making.[7] They listen curiously, aware that another's cultural expression has multiple layers and complexities. Such action parallels Marissa Silverman's concept of "listening-for," which necessitates active involvement and both "conveys and embodies empathy and compassion."[8] Listening for the not-already-known involves acknowledging one's own limited understandings. In Silverman's words, "When we listen to our own voice against the voices of others, we learn to realize how much we depend on our relationships with those around us."[9] As such, dialogic affective flows resist the building of musical communities on one-dimensional stories, including aforementioned narratives about individuals overcoming adversity.

This definition of dialogic affective flows parallels Hartmut Rosa's writings about resonant exchanges. In resonant relations, one entity vibrates, another responds, and the cycle repeats. Both parties must express themselves independently rather than merely echoing each other. In Rosa's words, "Resonant relationships require that both subject and world be sufficiently 'closed' or self-consistent so as to each speak in their own voice."[10] Each entity's own voice persists, resisting assimilation. Stated differently, those engaging in affective dialogue recognize and react to each other. Such interactions contrast sociologist Sherry Turkle's observation that youth often perceive friendship as one-sided: "It is a place for them to broadcast. It is not a place for them to listen. And there isn't an emotional level. You just have to have someone there."[11]

Additionally, dialogic affective flows can involve the rejection of perceptions others bring to the exchange. For example, a student may define themselves partly via opposition to labels such as *woman* or *Latinx*.[12] When fellow students and teachers respond with deference to requests to forgo or adopt certain labels, they facilitate the independent self-definition needed for dialogic affective flows. Dialogic affective flows thus necessitate openness to contradiction and moments in which the absence of resonant vibrations can inform altered understandings.

Consider how I (writing aligned right) might dialogically engage with a line from Mojave American Natalie Diaz's poem "Duned" (aligned left):

The land of Death is a duned land. Xeric. Saly'aay. Saly'aat. *We burn our dead*
we say—: because we do. *Touch me* I say, because it's a story we become.

[Pause]
Xe-ric? Sal-y'-aa-y? Saly'-att? Pronunciation?
[Annoyed, confused affects]

Xeric. Saly'aay. Saly'aat.

I feel excluded. On the outside.
Like students, when I say "hegemony"?
My dominant language excludes, erases, annihilates
[Sad, angry, shameful affects]
[Hesitation]

Xeric. Saly'aay. Saly'aat.

Grateful that these words live on
[Joyful affects]

Xeric. Saly'aay. Saly'aat.

Despite my cultural imperialism
[Frustrated and anxious affects]

We burn our dead we say—: because
we do.

Ephemeral human life
Respect into nothingness

we do.

Inevitable oblivion

Touch me I say

[Sustained Pause]
Desire, sensation
Yearning for closeness with others

Touch me I say

Release from alienation
[Excited, hopeful affects]

it's a story we become

I am not "we"
My own story insignificant

we become

Temporary solace in possibilities
Solace or resignation to the impossible?
[Mournful affects]

This example illustrates that dialogic affective flows often involve personal transformation. Beginning with self-centered concerns about my own exclusion from Mojave words, I transform through becoming saddened by and ashamed of my own culpability in their marginalized status. I change as I oscillate between feelings of excitement and sorrow upon engaging with the haunting and beautiful image of touching a fellow human while imagining their death and cremation.

Notice how the dialogic affects move back and forth in a web-like manner. Spiders begin with anchored endpoints and then work inward to form a balanced circular pattern; each section of the continually evolving web connects with and contributes to the overall arrangement. The whole is pieced together through inward motion. Similarly, the dialogic affective flows above include moments of repetition and hesitation rather than relentless expansion.

While both dialogic affective flows and the playful affective flows described in chapter 5 resist expansion and remain open to transformation, they differ in significant ways. First, dialogic affective flows necessitate a persistent slowing down in order to engage more fully with another's voice; they also demand a sustained back-and-forth exchange between entities. Playful affective flows are typically more momentary and unpredictable. They rely on a self-focused continued desire to engage rather than the aim of mutual recognition.

Second, playful affective flows can be their own ends; participants need not seek anything beyond the playful present moment. Conversely, students and teachers engage in dialogic affective flows in order to gain knowledge, skills, and dispositions needed for collective action with diverse others. What happens when dialogic affective flows occur among largely homogeneous student populations?

POLITICS OF DIALOGIC AFFECTIVE FLOWS

While schools, particularly public schools, remain one of the most diverse environments many individuals encounter over the course of their lives, schools typically represent neither national nor local diversity.[13] Through exclusionary housing practices, individuals and families remain geographically separated from members of other classes, races, and ethnicities. Additionally, neighbors can separate their children from those with contrasting religious beliefs, abilities, and privileges by enrolling them in private or charter schools.

Within already divided schools, an overrepresentation of white, higher socioeconomic status students typically constitute elective music classes.[14] The same holds true for community music making, which often relies on fees and transportation that inhibit lower socioeconomic class students from participating at the same rate as higher socioeconomic class students. Music students may therefore have few opportunities to interact directly with individuals who possess markedly different ideologies, cultures, and capitalism-related experiences than themselves.

Fostering dialogic affective flows necessitates questioning how resource distribution affects who is included in music-making endeavors. These resources include everything from food and shelter to musical instrument access to leisure time. Material resources may be distributed inequitably based on factors such as redlining, which involves limiting access to credit and other goods for individuals in areas deemed poor or hazardous; disparities can also result from teachers' choices. For instance, an educator may deny a student access to a certain instrument because of financial situation or disability. Inventing music electives that are accessible and desirable to diverse students, including those from lower socioeconomic class families, can encourage the dialogic affective flows important for resisting capitalist inequities.

Even when students have opportunities to interact with diverse others, asking students from historically marginalized backgrounds to share their stories places an added burden on those individuals.[15] As exemplified by my engagement with Diaz's poem, artistic endeavors created by historically marginalized individuals and groups can provide opportunities for dialogic affective flows that do not task students with educating their teachers and peers. As such, dialogic affective flows with existing music, art, and literary resources can reveal information about capitalist inequities without demanding added labor from students and community members experiencing such ills.

However, regardless of whether they involve engagement with people or with artistic practices, dialogic affective flows do not necessarily raise awareness about material inequities. Feminist philosopher Lisbeth Lipari explains, "There is thus a politics of listening, and it relates to who speaks and who doesn't, what is and is not said, how what is said is said, as well as, of course, to whom it is said and what is and is not heard, and *how* what is heard is heard."[16] Both overstructured and unstructured exchanges may undermine the centering of material inequities.

Paulo Freire and Donaldo Macedo note that inattention to content occurs when teachers overstructure discussions by primarily focusing on how much speaking time students receive. In such moments, teachers and students "overemphasize the process of turn-taking while de-emphasizing the critical apprehension of the object of knowledge."[17] It follows that when teachers and students focus on quantities of dialogic affective flows, they omit important considerations about the content and quality of such practices.

Turn taking itself can transform into a competitive capitalist practice, with each voice trying to trump others. Students can respond to peers by showing how they differ from them, thus building and reinforcing their own brand. One could, for instance, dialogue with Diaz's poem by making reference to obscure poems, which would promote their brand as a literary scholar. More broadly, while dialogic affective flows necessitate individuals' unique perspectives, too much focus on one's own voice can undermine opportunities for collective understanding and compromise.

Alternatively, unstructured affective dialogue problematically avoids teacher intervention. For example, a student might skip over the unfamiliar Mojave words while fixating on how the burning of deceased community members reminds them of a grandparent's funeral. Although this association may serve as a fine starting place, further sustained personal reflection will not necessarily cause the student to develop awareness about how settler colonial capitalism decimated Mojave culture and caused the extermination of countless native peoples.

Additionally, the content of both overstructured and unstructured dialogic affective flows can include false information. A student could respond to Diaz's poem with the unfounded assumption that the Mojave and other Indigenous peoples are rich from casino income or with inaccurate statements about life on tribal lands. While the student may feel moved by the poem, their incorrect perceptions inhibit understandings key for addressing the documented material inequities that the Mojave continue to face as a result of settler colonial capitalist practices.

In short, absent teacher intervention, the content of dialogic affective exchanges can reinforce individualistic attitudes, existing narratives, and false claims. Dialogic affective flows that contribute to resisting capitalist inequities necessitate that teachers question and guide students rather than merely relinquish authority.[18] The practice of witnessing material inequities centers such action.

WITNESSING MATERIAL INEQUITIES

Witnessing involves considering the potential ethical demands of artists and art making. Education philosophers David Hansen and Rebecca Sullivan explain that bearing witness involves understanding other people and phenomena as meriting ethical regard.[19] Witnessing "implies an underlying if unspoken respect for dignity in the *treatment* of fellow beings, and an abiding compassion for the human condition."[20] For example, a student bearing witness to a singer-songwriter's stories of depression would recognize these musical expressions not just as indications of the musician's humanity but as ethical demands in need of a social response. While not all musical expression requires an ethical reaction, witnessing begins with the assumption that it may.

Moreover, witnessing involves a sustained attempt to uncover realities of which one does not assume knowledge in advance. Witnesses "presume—or discover—that reality can be hard to see, to heed, and to keep present."[21] Importantly, witnessing material inequities necessitates focusing on facts rather than assumptions or opinions. Sullivan and Hansen explain "eye witnessing" as a key component of witnessing.[22] Eye witnessing "denotes a commitment to accuracy in fact and detail"; it involves rigor and sustained devotion to avoid distortion.[23]

Consider, for example, music teaching and learning in a community facing a proposal for the construction of a new freeway. Educators might begin with Kelly Bylica's listening project, in which students record sounds from their home environment and use them as the basis of a composition.[24] Next, students could search for sounds of freeways as well as research their sonic impacts, including on bird and animal resonances. Students could alter their compositions to reflect those potential changes in their environment's sounds. Subsequently, they could seek out possible benefits of the freeway, including local economic ones, and add a section to their composition reflecting those possibilities. Importantly, attention to possible changes in the local soundscape and communal benefits derive from the rigorous gathering of facts rather than social media opinions or other unconfirmed information.

Witnessing material inequities means naming their causes, including economic ones. As Nancy Fraser explains, the capitalist social order involves not only the economy but also "activities, relations, and processes defined as noneconomic, that make the economy possible."[25] For instance, a student might witness that members of their coastal community lack shelter because a massive storm damaged their homes. The student might name global warming as a key contributor to the storm and, hence, the lack of housing. Global warming results not just from individuals' choices but also from concerted economic efforts that worsen pollution and deplete resources. Capitalist expansion and exploitation directly contribute to global warming and thus to more intense weather patterns. Teachers and students might therefore name the link between capitalism, global warming, and local devastation.

Centering material inequities and their foundational economic causes avoids situations in which qualities such as race and gender serve to divide the working class. As argued throughout this text, racism, sexism, and other unjust systems should not go unacknowledged. However, there exists a difference in, for example, understanding the material inequity Louis Armstrong experienced during his childhood as a product solely of his race versus as a product of a capitalist system dependent on racial inequities. By witnessing the latter, teachers and students can come to understand the centrality of racism to past and present capitalist practices.

In addition to facts, bearing witness involves a commitment to detail. Writing about critical listening, Dylan Robinson describes that xwélalà:m, the Halq'eméylem word for listening, is "better understood as 'witness attentiveness.'"[26] He continues, "In xwélalà:m, witnesses are asked to document the knowledge and history being shared in the equivalent amount of detail to a book."[27] Similarly, Hansen and Sullivan write that witnessing involves copious notes and detailed descriptions;[28] the witness is "mindful of pertinent facts—they respect accuracy in even the tiniest details—and seeks to assemble the richest background knowledge possible."[29] In short, witnesses attend to facticity as well as the quality and quantity of detail.

Consider my attempt to bear witness dialogically with Kendrick Lamar's song "The Blacker the Berry." After listening to the full song, I selected lyrics I felt called to witness (left) and shared my witnessing (right):

You hate my people, your plan is to terminate my culture

(sad affects)

Witnessing the exclusion of Black culture and Black bodies from the music-making spaces I inhabit. Witnessing my ongoing complicity and the need for changed actions.

And man a say they put me inna chains, cah' we black

(disappointment; frustrated affects)

My own schooling taught that chains were a thing of the past. Witnessing that the effects of slavery and racial segregation are alive and well today.

(Pause for fact finding)

Eye witnessing that the median Black household has a net worth of $24,000, as compared to $188,000 for white households.[30]

You sabotage my community, makin' a killin'

(angry affects)

Acknowledging the Black, Brown, Indigenous, and Asian bodies that disproportionately produce and suffer for what white bodies consume.

(greater anger)

Witnessing racialized capitalism.

In order to challenge my own tendency to avoid discomfort, I then engaged with a couple of lyrics (left) that I (right) initially found troubling:

You're fuckin' evil I want you to recognize that I'm a proud monkey

(ashamed affects)

Witnessing Lamar's anger. I was taught never to curse; my parents implied that such language was lower class. In witnessing, I fuckin' reject that position. I do not pretend to take on his anger, but I can witness its legitimacy.

Proud monkey

Witnessing Lamar's joy and resilience; he appropriates a racial insult to serve his own ends. Honoring the power of someone claiming their individual and collective identity.

When gang banging make me kill a nigga blacker than me?

(uncertain affects)

Questioning how to bear witness to violence.

(hesitate)

(finding facts)

Eye witnessing that Black men make up 13 percent of the United States
population but 40 percent of the incarcerated population.[31] Witnessing
the rareness of upper-class individuals being incarcerated. Witnessing
that the world could be otherwise.
(momentary hope; discomfort)
Still questioning how to bear witness to violence. Remembering
that an Indiana University colleague, Quentin Wheeler-Bell, told
me that if you have not had to fight, then you are extremely
privileged. Witnessing that fighting can be a fuckin' necessity, and
my own unearned privilege reinforces that necessity for others.
Witnessing my complicity in this violence. Why have I made
this about me?
(pause)
Decentering I
(I) witness imperfectly.

Witnessing should not be understood as conclusive, especially when the eyewitness has not directly experienced the particular material inequity. Hansen and Sullivan acknowledge that there is no final or exhaustive witnessing and that even conscientious witnesses are fallible.[32] When bearing witness, the ongoing search to understand material conditions takes precedence over ease, assumptions, and conclusions.

Ultimately, the witness needs to make decisions about how to portray accumulated factual information. Hansen and Sullivan note: "The witness seeks to put forward the right details, at the right time, and in the right way. They cultivate and practice their judgment in discerning details that 'speak.'"[33] Portraying one's witnessing means selecting feelingful details that speak to the inequities at hand. As Robinson notes, xwélalà:m involves sharing "through the detail of feeling beyond fact."[34] In music education, such witnessing could involve decisions not only about what music to make and perform but also about who is welcomed and what type of communal space is nurtured, including potential affective flows.

Without further consideration, those bearing witness might bring diverse cultural practices into largely white, Eurocentric, middle-class music education spaces. Such action further marginalizes and minimizes various forms of music making and communication. This is not to say that Western art music making can never encourage witnessing. Take, for example, Alan Hovhaness's piece *And God Created Great Whales,* which witnesses the potential extinction of whales, or the West–Eastern Divan Orchestra, which Argentinean

Israeli conductor Daniel Barenboim and Palestinian scholar Edward Said created with the aim of witnessing "an alternative way to address the Israeli-Palestinian conflict."[35] However, musical notation, Western concert spaces, and silent audiences should not be the assumed starting places for witnessing engagements.[36]

Yet even thoughtfully considered solo witnessing of material inequities can reinforce the self-centeredness and capitalist individualism decried above. Drawing on Aristotelian ethics, philosopher Alasdair MacIntyre explains that when working to address capitalist ills, often "the question to be answered is not 'How am I to act?', but 'How are we to act?', just because what is at stake is a common good and not just the goods of individuals."[37] As such, music educators and students might focus on working together to collectively witness material inequities.

RELATIONAL WITNESSING

Imagine tasking students with cooperatively setting part of a poem written by someone who grew up in a low socioeconomic status household to music. Perhaps they collectively choose this excerpt from Amanda Gorman's poem "Monomyth": "Somewhere a reader reads this. Does resolution exist if it is ongoing, unwritten, unread? The part of the narrative where we see our hero as they see the world. We understand 'normal' in terms of how we believe a story begins. Inspirational, insightful, inside us. There is always someone missing from the music." The students work in groups to research Gorman's background, finding that she was raised by a single mother and has an auditory processing disorder. They might seek out information about the percentages of both children with single parents and those with disabilities who experience poverty. In order to avoid deficit narratives, they might acknowledge that Gorman's Harvard education and poetic fame have provided her substantial privileges and consider the role that Black joy plays in her life as well as their own.[38]

The students might then debate how to witness the confluence of joy, inequities, and privileges. They could ponder the following questions: What affects might the music they create aim to incite, and when during the poem should these affective moments occur? What timbres and rhythms might support this portrayal? What are the sounds of Los Angeles, where Gorman grew up, or Boston, where she attended school? Who in the classroom and local community has had similar experiences, and when might those voices come forward? While this endeavor may appear comprehensive thus far, in practice, further considerations are needed.

Without added attention, students may focus on evaluating Gorman as good or bad as well as classifying themselves and their classmates in terms of privilege or lack thereof. Philosopher Elizabeth Anderson problematizes educative practices that center what she terms second-order moral claims, including "Who is good or bad?" and "Who is better than who?"[39] In the aforementioned scenario, students might deem Gorman a good role model yet feel justified in understanding a struggling Black classmate as bad or unsuccessful. Focusing on people rather than systemic problems can foster divides between individuals and groups that undermine opportunities for collaborative action.

Alternatively, Anderson suggests emphasizing the first-order moral claims "What is our problem?" and "What should we do?" Engagement with these questions foregrounds cooperation and shared responsibility.[40] Drawing inspiration from Gorman's phrase "There is always someone missing from the music," perhaps the students collaboratively grapple with who is missing from their class and local musical communities. They might interrogate why those individuals are excluded, thus identifying "our problem." Next, they could extend their experimentation with sounds from Gorman's locales to music making and other aural phenomena in their immediate community attentive to those exclusions. Such explorations can result in a musical event responding to the question "What should we do about those missing from the music?"

Although Anderson's questions provide a way of initiating productive cooperative interactions, they necessitate the existence of an "our" and "we." While some classrooms may lend themselves to the formation of an "our" in which all voices have equal weight, other teaching and learning spaces risk divisions and silencing. Elizabeth Ellsworth explains how despite aiming for her collegiate class to unite around shared forms of oppression, students divided themselves around qualities such as race, gender, and nationality.[41] More broadly, Elizabeth Gould critiques understandings of democracy that rely on majority preferences, noting that such engagements overrule those in the minority.[42] When students arrive at "our" problem by omitting the voices of some classmates, they learn little about the discord inherent in meaningful collaboration, including discord with the potential to challenge capitalist inequities.

Hansen and Sullivan understand bearing witness as a calling, arguing that teachers cannot force students to bear witness.[43] Instead of compelling all students to bear witness to Gorman's poem or another agreed-on text, classes witnessing material inequities might remain open to forming affinity groups around areas of particular concern. Such action enables otherwise silenced forms of witnessing to arise. For example, drawing inspiration from the racial aspects of material inequities Gorman experienced, a group of Black, Brown, and Indigenous students may create music illuminating police brutality or other race-related issues. Alternatively, a group of female students may find meaning in focusing on the relationship between gender and inequity, sampling works from female and nonbinary music makers or poking fun at stereotypical male musical expressions. Some students may decide that they do not feel called to witness Gorman's text and thus seek out another school-appropriate poem.

When students enter affinity groups full of curiosity, intention, and willingness to be transformed, they have the potential to experience resonance. Rosa explains that resonance occurs when "students approach the material openly with a willingness to engage with it and be moved by it and trust that they can make it speak."[44] As such, affinity groups offer an alternative to alienating situations in which students forced into class-wide endeavors find subject matter unappealing or have nothing to say about it.[45]

Affinity groups also provide opportunities to resist extractive practices. Colonists' insatiable desire for resources was key to the propagation of global capitalism. This desire led to the stealing and colonizing of land tended by native inhabitants, often alongside the enslavement or extermination of those individuals. Colonizers often tried to force remaining Indigenous individuals to relinquish their cultural practices.

Robinson explains the phenomenon he terms "hungry listening" as a continuation of colonialist theft. Like colonists "starving for gold," contemporary non-Indigenous individuals engage in hungry listening by aiming to extract rather than exterminate cultural practices.[46] Such action sustains a settler colonialist mentality that understands possession as a right of those with privilege.[47] Similarly, when material inequities and accompanying power imbalances exist between students engaging in witnessing practices, exchanges can become a form of extraction in which more privileged individuals take information freely, without permission.

If Indigenous students or students from other historically marginalized groups wish to form affinity groups that resist unnecessary intrusion from teachers and peers, then music educators might provide them the resources to do so. As Robinson explains, Indigenous music practices may necessitate "spaces outside of the hungry settler gaze."[48] Likewise, students engaging in Black joy–centered music making may desire space to develop identities apart from peer observation and intrusion. Damaris Dunn and Bettina Love write that teachers promote Black joy when they facilitate a learning space that "allows Black children to imagine, dream, create, resist, take up space, and be. They get to define themselves on their own terms, free from interruption and prescriptive identity markers placed on Black folx."[49] This does not mean that educators should avoid providing constructive feedback or promote sustained segregation within their classroom. Rather, teachers and students can engage in thoughtful dialogue about how and what students might share with their class and local communities instead of defaulting to the "Western demand for complete accessibility."[50]

Affinity groups may assist students in developing collective voices that contribute to larger communal conversations, but they resist the class cohesiveness needed to challenge those at the top of capitalist pyramidal structures. Ellsworth explains that through exclusion of others, each affinity group's aims are inevitably partial and incomplete.[51] Additionally, while affinity groups at times enable the mutual recognition necessary for resonance, they ultimately undermine possibilities for the adaptive transformation key to resonance. Rosa argues that when individuals avoid dissonant interactions with those from other cultural or social backgrounds, they do so "at the price of confusing harmony for resonance and thus forfeiting the possibility of adaptive transformation."[52] Understanding often begins with not understanding, including by being misunderstood.[53]

Given the problems and possibilities of affinity groups, I propose that music teachers and students bearing witness to material inequities work in a middle ground between affinity groups and full communal engagement. Although educators cannot compel students to bear witness, they can encourage collaboration, particularly around broad areas of concern. In John Dewey's words, collective engagement "demands liberation of the potentialities of members of a group in harmony with the interests and goods which are common."[54] The group works toward collective interests while honoring the divergent perspectives and assets of group members, particularly those who have the most direct experiences with material inequities.

Group members might therefore aim for interdependence rather than either independence or assimilation. Stated differently, students engaged in cooperative witnessing cannot expect to fully understand or agree with others. Although working in the middle ground between affinity groups and full communal engagement is messy and complicated, it encourages students to develop skills and dispositions important for collaborative actions that resist capitalist inequities.

FROM RESISTING TO CHALLENGING, AND BACK AGAIN

In this chapter, I argue that dialogic affective flows with peers and with artistic endeavors can assist students in working with diverse others. These practices can transfer to communal endeavors, such as civic organizing, that contribute to the challenging of capitalist inequities throughout students' lives. Moreover, focusing on music making that cooperatively bears witness to material inequities can resist capitalism by revealing and foregrounding key communal problems in need of addressing.

The idea that music educators and students can artistically incite communal awareness about material inequities is empowering. Yet these practices constitute only initial steps in challenging capitalist ills. Absent acknowledging the embryonic nature of resisting endeavors within teaching and learning spaces, music makers may adopt self-congratulatory attitudes that inhibit further action.

Many of the skills and processes addressed in this chapter may contribute to more directly confronting capitalist ills, as described in the next chapter. Why, then, might music educators and students foster dispositions that may eventually contribute to the addressing of capitalist inequities rather than challenge them more directly? My response is twofold.

First, many music educators work in schools and communities in which the direct challenging of capitalist inequities would face intense criticism from stakeholders, possibly resulting in terminated employment. In such instances, music educators may logically decide to retain their jobs by focusing on resisting capitalist ills rather than overtly challenging them. Although resisting capitalist inequities may result in pushback from students, parents, and other community members who wish to retain the music education status quo, teachers might decide that their own values and convictions outweigh such adversity. They will likely not face terminated employment for resisting-related practices sensitive to their community's values.

Second, while directly challenging capitalist inequities may have a more immediate impact, it does not necessarily prepare students for the ways in which they might collaboratively address such issues in the long term. For example, a student focused on challenging capitalist inequities through disruptive artistic events might not develop the skills and dispositions needed to collaborate within workers' unions or other organizations comprised of diverse individuals. Whether learning related to resisting or directly challenging capitalism proves more impactful for students and their communities in the long run varies based on local circumstances, including future ones that teachers and students cannot necessarily predict.

In summary, dialogic relational witnessing provides music educators and students opportunities for resonant transformation. It is a collective singing that is not always in unison. In the most promising moments, such practices foster agreement about what capitalism-related problems a temporary "we" might resist.

In the spirit of *Choose Your Own Adventure* books, to investigate challenging capitalist inequities, continue onto chapter 7. Alternatively, examine how music educators can facilitate students' thriving within capitalist economies by turning to chapter 4, or investigate playful surviving under capitalism by reading chapter 5.

NOTES

1. Silvia Federici, *Patriarchy of the Wage: Notes on Marx, Gender, and Feminism* (Brooklyn: PM Press, 2021), 67.

2. William Cheng, *Loving Music Till It Hurts* (New York: Oxford University Press, 2019), 107.

3. Cheng, *Loving Music Till It Hurts*, 126.

4. Cheng, *Loving Music Till It Hurts*, 59.

5. Maxine Greene, "Imagining Futures: The Public School and Possibility," *Journal of Curriculum Studies* 32, no. 2 (2000): 274.

6. Antonio R. Damasio, *The Feeling of What Happens: Body and Emotion in the Making of Consciousness* (Orlando: Harcourt, 1999).

7. I understand *dignity* and *respect* as Elizabeth Anderson explains, acting in "relations of equality." Anderson describes that functioning in "relations of equality" involves listening and dialogue undergirded by "mutual consultation, reciprocation, and recognition." Elizabeth Anderson, "What Is the Point of Equality?" *Ethics* 109, no. 2 (January 1999): 313.

8. Marissa Silverman, "Listening-for Social Justice," in *Giving Voice to Democracy in Music Education*, ed. Lisa C. DeLorenzo (New York: Routledge, 2015), 161.

9. Silverman, "Listening-for Social Justice," 164.

10. Hartmut Rosa, *Resonance: A Sociology of Our Relationship to the World*, trans. James C. Wagner (Cambridge: Polity Press, 2019), 174.

11. Sherry Turkle, *Reclaiming Conversation: The Power of Talk in a Digital Age* (New York: Penguin Books, 2015), 163.

12. Elizabeth Ellsworth, "Why Doesn't This Feel Empowering? Working through the Repressive Myths of Critical Pedagogy," *Harvard Educational Review* 59, no. 3 (1989): 311.

13. Emma García, "Schools Are Still Segregated, and Black Children Are Paying a Price," *Economic Policy Institute*, February 12, 2020, https://www.epi.org/publication/schools-are-still-segregated-and-black-children-are-paying-a-price/.

14. Kenneth Elpus and Carlos R. Abril, "Who Enrolls in High School Music? A National Profile of U.S. Students, 2009–2013," *Journal of Research in Music Education* 67, no. 3 (2019): 323–38.

15. Juliet Hess, "'Putting a Face on It': The Trouble with Storytelling for Social Justice in Music Education," *Philosophy of Music Education Review* 29, no. 1 (2021): 67–87.

16. Lisbeth Lipari, *Listening, Thinking, Being: Toward an Ethics of Attunement* (University Park: Pennsylvania State University Press, 2014), 53.

17. Paulo Freire and Donaldo P. Macedo, "A Dialogue: Culture, Language, and Race," *Harvard Educational Review* 65, no. 3 (1995): 383.

18. Freire and Macedo, "Dialogue," 383.

19. David T. Hansen and Rebecca Sullivan, "What Renders a Witness Trustworthy? Ethical and Curricular Notes on a Mode of Educational Inquiry," *Studies in Philosophy and Education* 41 (2022): 156–7.

20. Hansen and Sullivan, "What Renders a Witness Trustworthy?" 157. Emphasis added.

21. Hansen and Sullivan, "What Renders a Witness Trustworthy?" 157.

22. Hansen and Sullivan, "What Renders a Witness Trustworthy?" 156.

23. Hansen and Sullivan, "What Renders a Witness Trustworthy?" 154–56.

24. Cathy Benedict, *Music and Social Justice: A Guide for Elementary Educators* (New York: Oxford University Press, 2021), 81–88.

25. Nancy Fraser, *Cannibal Capitalism: How Our System Is Devouring Democracy, Care, and the Planet—and What We Can Do about It* (Brooklyn: Verso Books, 2022), 82.

26. Dylan Robinson, *Hungry Listening: Resonant Theory for Indigenous Sound Studies* (Minneapolis: University of Minnesota Press, 2020), 52.

27. Robinson, *Hungry Listening*, 52.

28. Hansen and Sullivan, "What Renders a Witness Trustworthy?" 154.

29. Hansen and Sullivan, "What Renders a Witness Trustworthy?" 165.

30. Palash Ghosh, "Black Americans Earn 30% Less Than White Americans, While Black Households Have Just One-Eight Wealth of White Households," *Forbes*, June 18, 2021, https://www.forbes.com/sites/palashghosh/2021/06/18/blacks-earn-30-less-than-whites-while-black-households-have-just-one-eighth-of-wealth-of-white-households/.

31. Özlem Sensoy and Robin, DiAngelo, *Is Everyone Really Equal? An Introduction to Key Concepts in Social Justice Education* (New York: Teachers College Press, 2017), 129.

32. Hansen and Sullivan, "What Renders a Witness Trustworthy?" 157.

33. Hansen and Sullivan, "What Renders a Witness Trustworthy?" 168.

34. Robinson, *Hungry Listening*, 52.

35. "The Founders," East-West Divan Orchestra, accessed February 28, 2024, https://west-eastern-divan.org/founders. I am grateful to an anonymous reviewer who provided these two suggestions.

36. In Robinson's words: "To challenge settler colonial perception requires reorienting the form by which we share knowledge, the way we convey the

experience of sound, song, and music. In an academic setting, this involves reorienting the normative places, flows, and relationships wherein we share this knowledge." Robinson, *Hungry Listening*, 15.

37. Alasdair MacIntyre, *Ethics in the Conflicts of Modernity: An Essay on Desire, Practical Reasoning, and Narrative* (Cambridge: Cambridge University Press, 2016), 72.

38. For a detailed discussion of Black joy, see Lindsey Stewart, *The Politics of Black Joy: Zora Neale Hurston and Neo-abolitionism* (Evanston, IL: Northwestern University Press, 2021).

39. Elizabeth Anderson, "Education for Democracy in an Age of Political Polarization," Philosophy of Education Society, March 4, 2023, video, 79:36, https://drive.google.com/file/d/1B1F1qlmnX3jZi69LSFy5dLB_40oBunAJ/.

40. Anderson, "Education for Democracy in an Age of Political Polarization."

41. Ellsworth, "Why Doesn't This Feel Empowering?" 317.

42. Elizabeth Gould, "Social Justice in Music Education: The Problematic of Democracy," *Music Education Research* 9, no. 2 (2007): 229–4.

43. Hansen and Sullivan, "What Renders a Witness Trustworthy?" 154.

44. Rosa, *Resonance*, 245.

45. Rosa, *Resonance*, 247.

46. Robinson, *Hungry Listening*, 48.

47. Robinson, *Hungry Listening*, 10.

48. Robinson, *Hungry Listening*, 34.

49. Damaris Dunn and Bettina L. Love, "Antiracist Language Arts Pedagogy Is Incomplete without Black Joy," *Racial Literacy: Implications for Curriculum, Pedagogy, and Policy* 1 (2021): 70.

50. Robinson, *Hungry Listening*, 21–22.

51. Ellsworth, "Why Doesn't This Feel Empowering?" 318.

52. Rosa, *Resonance*, 363.

53. Lipari, *Listening, Thinking, Being*, 140.

54. John Dewey, *The Public and Its Problems* (Athens, OH: Swallow Press, 1927), 147.

SEVEN

CHALLENGING CAPITALIST MATERIAL INEQUITIES THROUGH RESPONSE-ABLE DISRUPTIONS

CAPITALIST PRACTICES RELY ON EVER-EXPENDING flows, including increases in material goods, virtual products, and social media followers. In music education, the unceasing accumulation of skills, resources, and competitive accolades mirrors and reinforces key capitalist flows and dispositions. Playful affective flows that circulate without expanding can provide a meaningful alternative to capitalist greed, but they do not directly confront key problems of contemporary capitalism, including material inequities reinforced through hierarchies based on class, disability, gender, and race. Dialogic affective flows can encourage the witnessing of material inequities and the cooperation key to civic actions that may eventually alter troubling aspects of capitalism. Yet since dialogic affective flows rarely incite immediate social change, music educators and students should understand how to more directly challenge capitalist ills, including the premise that societies necessitate economic losers.

In considering what types of affective flows directly challenge capitalist inequities, I begin with what might appear to be an uncontroversial premise: Challenging problematic aspects of contemporary economic practices necessitates disruption. Indeed, it is hard to imagine how any system, be it classroom routines or legal rights, can change without disruptive moments that temporarily cease habitual actions. In contrast with capitalist growth and accumulation, disruptive affective flows

halt
UNSETTLE the
e as e of con tin u ed
consumption and

its Re sul TinG
InE quiTIEs

However, disruptions can serve capitalist aims just as easily as they can thwart them. Take, for example, my poetic attempt at fostering

DISRUPTION.
Did you STOP? And WONDER?
Why I
SHOUTED
If only I could keep going
MAKE THE TEXT BIGGER
BIGGER
DO YOU STILL SEE THE CAPITALS?
MAYBE BOLDFACE WILL HELP
Or writing over here
CAPITAL, BOLD, ALIGN RIGHT
I FORGOT TO ENLARGE

<u>MORE DiSRUPtioN</u>

What happens when the disruption subsides?
Do you desire more?
Please purchase this poem!

Before considering what qualities of disruption might challenge problematic aspects of capitalism, I examine the nature of disruptive affective flows more broadly.

DISRUPTIVE AFFECTIVE FLOWS

Artistic endeavors have the potential to disrupt individuals' often unquestioned acceptance of their current situation. Theodore Adorno argued that art should foster "refusal" to accept sociopolitical economic practices and inequities.[1] Through such artistic encounters, "the untruth of the social situation comes to light."[2] For instance, engaging with a disruptive sequence of grinding dissonances can jolt listeners from complacency, encouraging awareness that standard musical patterns—like sociopolitical economic practices more broadly—are contingent and can undergo alterations.

Despite Adorno's flawed focus on specific music genres he thought could produce heightened critical awareness, including the atonal music of his contemporaries Alban Berg and Arnold Schoenberg, he also hinted that certain qualities of music making could unsettle individuals' passive acceptance of their socioeconomic positionality.[3] He argued: "The ugly must constitute, or be able to constitute, an element of art."[4] Building on Adorno's work, cultural theorist Sianne Ngai proposes that artistic endeavors can produce certain types of "ugly feelings" that disrupt individuals' self-conceptions, including regarding their economic positionality.[5]

According to Ngai, ugly feelings can include anxiety, paranoia, and envy. Common to the experience of such feelings is a sense of unease and confusion. Ugly feelings involve moments of inactivity, disorientation, and bewilderment.[6] Ngai adds that ugly feelings tend to "produce an unpleasurable feeling *about* the feeling."[7] For instance, when an artistic endeavor encourages one to feel anxious, the participant may intuit, "I feel an unpleasant sense of anxiousness." While one may feel anxious about an event they interpret as pleasant, such as performing a musical solo, the ugly feeling of anxiousness occurs through a coupling of bewildering anxiety and discomfort.

The unpleasantness that coincides with ugly feelings occurs partly because ugly feelings are "saturated with socially stigmatizing meanings and values."[8] For example, imagine a pop song that, rather than encouraging listeners to imagine themselves as ultrarich, incites envy for the ultrarich. Given the association of envy with pettiness, individuals in capitalist societies are generally socialized not to celebrate envying another's riches. Those experiencing the ugly feeling of envy might therefore recoil in response to the stigma associated with it. When noticed and interrogated, such recoiling can temporarily disrupt taken-for-granted ways of being in the world. Students reflecting on why they recoil at the experience of envying the ultrarich might come to problematize unrestrained material consumption made possible through global inequalities and natural resource decimation.

Emphasizing ugly feelings alone, however, does not account for how music making with other qualities can encourage disruption. An angry, mournful, or harmonious protest song could incite temporary disruptive recoiling that encourages reflecting on and maybe even responding to problematic aspects of contemporary capitalism. Extending Ngai's work, I propose centering disruptive affective flows, which can include ugly feelings as well as other affects that encourage critical reflection. Disruptive affective flows involve a

break

Halting, interruption,
Discontinuity

Artistic endeavors that
S T O P
participants from
COnTiNuING
Resist NOrM al
provoke
di S jUnc tIOn
ARresting
!
?

Since Ngai, like Adorno, explains ugly feelings as existing within artistic works, she does not account for potentially divergent experiences of different listeners. While one person could listen to Beyoncé's "Formation" and experience the ugly feeling of anxiety, another listener could experience joy and a third anger. Certain musical endeavors may tend to invoke ugly feelings, but participants' unique prior encounters and current contexts will contribute to their affective experiences.

Ugly feelings may serve as a starting point for disruptive artistic endeavors that can challenge capitalist inequities, but teachers and students might also attend to disruptive affective flows more broadly, including those incited by pedagogical efforts.

A SU DDE N
(pause)
inTRuSiOn. An
un pLAnn ed emotional OUT
B U RST . An expression
terror, disgust, res igna tion. . .
is an EVER PreseNT possiBIL
ITY!
YET, AS THIS WRITING EXERCISE DEMONSTRATES,
DISRUPTION
Can still RESIST
POLITICAL
action.
CONTINUED disruption
BECOMES CoMmoN pLAcE AND **UN**
seen.

D isruption can also serve capitalist ends and aims.

DISRUPTION AND CAPITALISM

Capitalism thrives on disruption. Globally, capitalist proponents have taken advantage of crises, including natural disasters and social upheavals, to implement what Naomi Klein describes as economic "shock therapy."[9] Detailing specific events in countries ranging from Chile to Poland to China, Klein explains how leaders enacted market friendly policies while destroying local social safety nets and individuals' life savings within a matter of days. What proponents of unrestrained capitalism fail to enact through incremental policy changes they accomplish via disruptive shocks, often while most citizens remain physically and emotionally distracted by social unrest or other predicaments.

Within industries, *disruption* has come to mean a process "whereby a smaller company with fewer resources is able to successfully challenge established incumbent businesses."[10] The smaller company attracts consumers overlooked by the incumbent company and then moves up market, attracting the incumbent's primary customer base. As Clayton Christensen, Michael Raynor, and Rory McDonald explain: "When mainstream customers start adopting the entrants' offerings in volume, disruption has occurred."[11] Disruption may lead to lower prices and better services for more consumers, but it can also result in monopoly-like control over production that encourages worker and consumer exploitation. In short, disruption does not necessarily challenge capitalist inequities, and it may even worsen them.

The constant flow of sensory information enabled by social media and other internet platforms means that selling commodities to contemporary consumers necessitates more grandiose disruptions. While in previous decades, scantily clad models in promotional materials may have sufficiently captured the attention needed for product promotion, the ubiquitous nature of such images encourages marketers to search for ever more arresting events. Take, for example, marketing related to the infamous Fyre Festival. Billed as a luxury music festival, the poorly organized event left most attendees sleeping on mattresses in tents designed for emergency disaster relief and fearing for their safety.

Festival organizers promoted the event through a brilliantly disruptive marketing strategy. They paid four hundred musicians, athletes, models, and actors to simultaneously post a single orange tile on Instagram, piquing the attention of curious social media followers, who clicked on the tile and viewed the Fyre promotional video.[12] While the promotional video itself would have likely gone unnoticed amid the flurry of everyday social media posts, the orange tiles provided a visual disruption that changed consumers' behavior, ultimately creating profit for festival organizers.

As capitalist politicians, producers, media corporations, and other powerful groups use ever more invasive disruptions to encourage certain behaviors, many twenty-first-century individuals have become partly immune to disruptions, including artistic ones. Hua Hsu explains that the "buffeting emotional weather of everyday life" encourages "the normalized exhaustion that comes with life in the new economy."[13] This emotional depletion can coincide with a desensitization to all but the most sensational of disruptions. As such, potentially disruptive artistic endeavors, ranging from Berg's atonal music to an opera invoking the ugly feeling of anxiety, may do little to awaken awareness of one's socioeconomic conditions.

If disruption is necessary but not sufficient for raising awareness about problematic aspects of capitalism, then the qualities of disruptions that reinforce rather than challenge capitalist ills necessitate attention. In order to consider the qualities of musical disruptions that most directly challenge capitalist ills, I compare the qualities of the procapitalist Fyre Festival promotional video with three potentially disruptive music videos that address capitalist inequities. As demonstrated by my dependence on YouTube videos, even disruptive music practices often rely on capitalist producers who profit handsomely from free or underpaid labor.[14]

QUALITIES OF DISRUPTION

One quality that might distinguish disruptions that reinforce versus challenge capitalist ideals is their speed. Capitalism thrives on a continual speeding up of commodity production. As Joseph Abramo notes, this has led to a dematerialization of cultural commodities.[15] For example, transactions like purchasing records, which used to necessitate paper money and physical products, now occur through digital currency and immediate online sound file transfers. Money circulates more quickly, creating a faster turnaround from production to profit for capitalist producers.

Similarly, consider the speeds within the aforementioned Fyre Festival promotional video. In the first forty seconds, the rapidly changing clips of supermodels, waves, and musicians average one to two seconds each. In the second half of the video, the images change multiple times per second. In tandem with the quicker succession of video clips comes faster music and more motion-filled images. Visuals of models walking, lying on the beach, and sipping cocktails give way to people running, jumping, swimming, and kissing. Starting with a single disruptive orange square, the continually increasing speed of the disruptive images maintains viewers' attention, thus making the ultimate ticket sale more likely.

Conversely, disruptive affective flows that challenge capitalist practices tend to remain steady or even slow down one's sense of time. U n set
t ling one's TA kE N for granted understandings of the world, including their economic positionality and its related values, necessitates not a moment of trouble but e v olv ing
dis
rup
TiVE
events. Like Donna Haraway's larger call to "stay with the trouble of living and dying in response-ability on a damaged earth,"[16] teachers and students who seek to disrupt their own and others' long-standing senses of self
s t a y
with the mom- ents that
avoid
res
o lut
io
n. . .

Disruptive artistic and pedagogical endeavors that sustain trouble often involve complexity and density that resist immediate gratification or clarity. For example, consider doctoral student Hollie Harding's climate change–focused piece titled *Melting, Shifting, Liquid World*.[17] Presented at the National Maritime Museum in London, the piece integrates sounds derived from publicly available ocean monitoring systems data and recordings of ice sheets melting. Participants walk among the musicians while listening to an electroacoustic tape via bone-conducting headphones, which transmit sound directly into the inner ear and enable the layering of other sounds. Such art making parallels Haraway's description of "staying with trouble" as involving "continuous weaving" as well as twisting, anchoring, and launching.[18] Lacking a consistent pulse, Harding's disruptive melding of eerie sound and performer-audience motion encourages a sensation of slowing, sustained anguish and lingering disruption.

Alternatively, consider an anticapitalist music video by British rapper and activist Lowkey.[19] While lyrics like "the kleptocracy orchestrate and subjugate, the corporate state that isn't freedom" have the potential to disrupt individuals' awareness of their economic emplacement, the consistent pulsing beat tends to maintain or even speed up a listener's sense of time. Additionally, rapidly changing images—which consist mainly of Lowkey singing alone, exercising, or performing for audiences—recall the quickness of the Fyre Festival promotional video. Although teachers might use such music making to create prolonged unsettling discussions about the limits of capitalism, the music itself resists the slowness needed for sustained troubling.

Likewise, consider music education practices that, while disruptive to long-standing music education traditions, speed up pedagogical pacing. For instance, leaders of Little Kids Rock (now rebranded as Music Will), which has disrupted exclusionary P-12 music education practices, emphasize the speed of music learning in their system. Their website states: "By emphasizing performance and composition over reading notes, students develop a musical voice and acquire musical skills at an accelerated pace."[20] While Music Will's modern band approach is still potentially valuable for other reasons, this emphasis on speedy learning aligns with the ever-increasing pace of capitalist growth.

A related second quality involves the trajectories incited by musical disruptions. Disruptions that expand outward from or enhance a stable sense of self tend to reinforce problematic aspects of capitalism. Conversely, disruptions that draw inward to self-reflection or even recoiling from external conditions have potential to illuminate capitalist ills. Consistent with Ngai's argument that ugly feelings involve "trajectories of repulsion," such flows destabilize one's sense of self as they encourage inward-looking disorientation.[21]

In *Melting, Shifting, Liquid World,* Harding fosters haunting, anxiety-laden sensations that circulate among musicians and audience-participants. Such artistic endeavors encourage audience-participants to look around and inward. Like a string figure bound by the limits of a single string, hesitant and repulsive affective flows turn in on themselves, creating new tangles and configurations absent accumulation or expansion.[22]

Alternatively, consider the Fyre Festival promotional video. Atop rapidly changing images of swimsuit-clad models, the voiceover states: "All these things that seem big and impossible are not; it gives people that type of energy, that type of power."[23] In this statement, the self does not develop or seek energy and power—energy and power augment and extend festival goers' current selves. This language implies outward-oriented, expansive trajectories that parallel ever-growing capitalist flows. In such affirming moments, inequities within one's local and global environments go unnoticed and unquestioned.

Similarly, the self-important lyrics and images of perfected muscular male bodies in Lowkey's aforementioned video promote a sense of self-righteousness for both artist and viewer that resists critical reflection. Such energized comradery can be used toward anticapitalist political ends, but the disruption itself mirrors self-interested, expansive affective flows that reinforce capitalism. The trajectories of disruptions promoting capitalist ideals reinforce and distract;

the trajectories of disruptions that may encourage a challenging of capitalist ills bewilder and unsettle.

Third, artistic disruptions that challenge capitalism tend to acknowledge the limits of art making. Ngai explains that the tolerance of art within capitalist markets "assumes its social ineffectuality or innocuousness."[24] If art making had more potential to undermine—rather than reinforce—capitalism, then it would receive more scrutiny. Yet both elitist and popular music making, including that with subversive sentiments, go largely unchallenged by capitalist producers.

It follows that the disruptive artistic endeavors with the most potential to directly challenge capitalism do not point to the arts as a solution. Music making that raises awareness about capitalist ills absent posing specific ways forward encourages participants to ponder their own complicity and passivity within capitalist systems. For example, Harding's installation leaves viewers with unsettling, anxious affects without a clear call to action. Such endeavors recall Ngai's statement that through the incitement of ugly feelings, "art thus comes to interrogate the problematically limited agency of art."[25] While questioning might not result in meaningful changes, awareness of one's current inaction often holds more potential to encourage altered behavior than musical disruptions that leave participants with an immediate sense of empowerment or accomplishment.

Unsurprisingly, disruptions that reinforce the self-interested dispositions key to capitalism often resolve through the purchasing of commodities, including artistic ones. In the case of Fyre Festival, the ultimate aim of the disruptive orange squares was for viewers to purchase festival tickets. Likewise, Lowkey's video urges listeners to "confront the culture of power with the power of culture," implying the benefits of purchasing music recordings and concert tickets. In both examples, art making is itself the solution.

Moreover, artistic endeavors emphasizing material realities—as opposed to cultural symbols or other abstract references—have potential to highlight their own limited agency. As David Harvey notes, challenging capitalism must involve challenging "the material processes whereby surpluses are both created and appropriated by capital."[26] While many individuals have some sense that the products they purchase rely on underpaid laborers working in poor and sometimes dangerous conditions, composing music for images alternating between contemporary capitalist excesses and workers producing goods under horrific working conditions can cause direct confrontation with exploitation and material inequities. Rather than providing a joyous conclusion, student composers might aim to bewilder audiences with ugly feelings such as anxiety.

These affective flows can encourage participants to acknowledge the limits of art making to address observed inequities.

While the three aforementioned qualities—slowness, inward trajectories, and lack of resolution—can assist music educators and students in selecting disruptive artistic endeavors with greater potential to challenge capitalist inequities, much music making fits in the vast middle ground between the two extremes of reinforcing versus challenging. Take, for example, DJ CAVEM's eco hip-hop music video "Sprout That Life."[27] Using a moderate tempo and typical hip-hop beats, the song and images move at a fairly constant pace, neither slowing nor speeding up. Many video clips foreground plants rather than humans, favoring botanical life over human self-aggrandizement. However, other clips center DJ CAVEM absent any greenery, and at multiple points in the video, DJ CAVEM deals out seed packs to parody the releasing of cash popular among hip-hop artists, which I interpret as a form of self-branding. The video points to healthy local eating as a resolution, while avoiding suggesting that the arts can solve capitalism-related problems.

Given potentially disruptive music making, music educators and students might consider how pedagogical decisions can further slowing, inward-focused, unresolved affective flows. While activities like reflective journaling and prolonged music creation can contribute to such affective flows, the nature of engagement necessitates ongoing attention. A single phrase

Experimented
Reborn
Rejected
Renewed
Brings slowness
H E S I
TAte
Surrender S t **O** p

Arts are
Are arts
No
Answers
Un Found

If artistic pedagogical endeavors alone do little to change the problematic aspects of contemporary globalized capitalism, then music educators and students might focus on the responses that arise from such endeavors.

RESPONSE-ABLE DISRUPTION

Acknowledging the limits of art making to challenge key aspects of capitalism risks music educators, students, and community members defaulting to a sense of cynicism and impossibility. One might logic that if artistic endeavors have minimal direct impact on material inequities, then why focus on such issues at all? More problematically, this line of reasoning can encourage understanding current capitalist practices as unchangeable, diminishing the possibilities for collective imagining and action. In Slajov Žižek's words: "The main function of ideological censorship today is not to crush actual resistance . . . but to crush hope."[28] Disruptive artistic endeavors that leave participants hopeless about the prospects of altering material circumstances further narratives about the inevitability of capitalist practices.

Alternatively, when music educators and students attend to the responses surrounding disruptive artistic endeavors, including pedagogical engagements and interactions at concerts and other community events, they can challenge passivity and defeatism. Recalling Haraway's aim of staying "with the trouble of living and dying in response-ability on a damaged earth,"[29] I offer that disruptive artistic endeavors demand both a response and a sense that one has the ability to make material changes.

The initial part of a response might involve simply showing where one stands on a controversial issue. Political scientist Clarissa Hayward argues that part of political disruption involves forcing "members of dominant groups to take sides."[30] Through this side taking, a disruptive artistic endeavor can cause the surfacing of issues individuals are motivated to ignore.

Hayward explains motivated ignorance as a way of being in the world in which individuals avoid investigating or acknowledging problematic aspects of contemporary social systems. Motivated ignorance enables individuals to maintain an understanding of themselves as good people who behave ethically.[31] For instance, I exhibit motivated ignorance when I avoid asking whether my white, middle-class background provided me advantages when competing for education and employment opportunities. Maintaining motivated ignorance encourages me to understand my successes as stemming from ethical hard work and perseverance while omitting the role inherited privilege played in my accomplishments.

Hayward proposes that successful political disruption occurs when individuals confront their own motivated ignorance.[32] Withdrawing motivated ignorance involves acknowledging structural inequities as well as refusing to cooperate with and, to the extent possible, within them.[33] A group of political actors who withdraw their cooperation from problematic ways of knowing and being creates disruptive situations in which others must confront their own motivated ignorance. Such disruptions compel another "subset of members of the public to pay attention to things that they are motivated to ignore."[34]

Take, for example, the musicians who brought attention to the shooting of an unarmed Black teenager by a white police officer by disrupting a St. Louis Symphony Orchestra concert with a surprise flash-mob style performance of "Justice for Mike Brown."[35] Quoting from Pete Seegar's song "Which Side Are You On?" the singers, embedded throughout the audience, momentarily refocused the audience's attention on the unjust killing.

Rather than educating the public about new issues, successful disruption often targets people who are familiar with the debate at hand but have chosen not to act in support of the cause. In the case of the St. Louis Symphony, since Mike Brown was killed in St. Louis, attendees likely possessed familiarity with the local tragedy. Hayward explains that by drawing on prior knowledge, disruptive events cause the surfacing of latent debates, such as whether police brutality against Black individuals is problematic. When done in a way that demands a public response, such action causes individuals not only to acknowledge a debate they were motivated to ignore but also to pick a side.[36] During "Justice for Mike Brown," the disruptive singing caused audience members to claim their side by either standing and clapping in support of the singers or averting their eyes.

Imagine if Harding added message boards or interactive computer stations to *Melting, Shifting, Liquid World*. Event participants might brainstorm what they could do to assist with the problems exposed through the music making as well as how elected officials and other institutional leaders should act in response. These responsive actions could be shared during and after the event as well as through larger equity focused movements, such as https://usvshate.org/.

Alternatively, imagine students composing and performing an anxiety-inducing piece addressing capitalist worker exploitation. The program could contain a QR code that links audience members to a survey. During the performance, audience members could be asked questions related to their experiences, perhaps including how the piece made them feel, whether they thought the working conditions portrayed through the piece were problematic, and why. A teacher or student could monitor the responses and share them with the full audience as appropriate.[37]

Through such response opportunities, participants metaphorically show their cards; they must take a stance on the issue, even if their response consists of a refusal to acknowledge the disruption. The public nature of these events means that fellow attendees will notice this refusal, causing participants to own their positionality in a visible, communal way. Response-oriented moments remove the choice of passive musical engagement.

Hayward argues that even if such disruptions do not result in widespread public sympathy, they may reach sympathetic actors who, jolted them from motivated ignorance, subsequently take advantage of opportunities to affect change.[38] They may vote, change hiring practices, engage in protests, take on political leadership, or pursue other actions. Additionally, Hayward notes that "disruptive politics shift public discourse. They put issues on the political agenda that previously were off."[39] The St. Louis Symphony disruption contributed to keeping systemic racism and police brutality in the public eye. By sustaining public attention on capitalist inequities, repeated disruptions can encourage more far-reaching public outcry, increasing the likelihood that political leaders and other stakeholders enact changes.

While these responses expose where students and community members stand on a specific issue, they can also reveal an overarching position on the question, Is change possible? Although teachers cannot necessarily alter the thinking of students or community members who do not want to see possibilities for change, having individuals take ownership of this position encourages them to reflect on their choice rather than assuming it as a given. Students, teachers, and community members who have defaulted to hopelessness or passivity may reconsider their positionality after gaining awareness that they can choose otherwise. Yet students and audience members cannot take a thoughtful position on issues they do not understand.

Interdisciplinary collaborations can provide music teachers and students opportunities to learn about capitalist inequities while ensuring that most class time involves music making. At the P-12 level, music educators and students might work alongside a history class investigating how colonization contributed to global wealth inequities or a science class looking at the relationship between resource depletion and climate change. Students could set music to accounts of people whose livelihoods are increasingly disrupted by droughts or imagine the perspectives of plants and animals facing extinction. In order to find or craft these accounts, music educators might collaborate with social studies, science, or English teachers. Art making thus becomes part of what Haraway explains as a "reknitted" order in which "human beings are with and of the earth."[40] Importantly, students' compositions would aim to invoke affective flows that create pause or interruption as opposed to sustained sadness that encourages a sense of defeat and hopelessness.

In these examples, the combination of int
Er
rUP **tive**
musical gestures and texts or images focused on Mater ial
realities exposes the motivated ignorance enabling capitalist inequities to persist. Yet such response-inducing endeavors do not propose art making as a solution to capitalist inequities.

At the collegiate level, endeavors might involve interschool collaborations. For instance, Harding worked alongside climate scientists, and a renowned nature sound engineer provided the recordings of ice sheets melting. Likewise, members of a sociology department could offer commentary about how human interactions create a problem addressed in a piece of music; an environmental studies program might display facts about climate change for a nature-focused concert. More broadly, historians, scientists, and other scholars can assist music makers in grounding their work in present contexts, while music makers can disruptively look toward the future with both warnings and imagined alternatives. Such interdisciplinary music making exemplifies Alain Badiou's claim that an artist aims "to be of one's time, through an unprecedented manner of not being in one's time . . . to have the courage to be untimely."[41]

In addition to responding, "response-ability" necessitates feeling capable of making change. Haraway emphasizes that the "ability" part of "response-ability" is necessarily collective and evolving rather than individualistic and static. Such thinking parallels physicist and feminist philosopher Karen Barad's conception of agency. Barad explains agency as emerging through the meeting of forces rather than as an inherent property of individuals.[42] This interpersonal, developing conception of ability and agency contrasts with the Fyre Festival promoters' claim that music making gives individuals energy and power.

Since collaborations often reveal ways forward that no individual could have imagined absent group input, how teachers and students are able to respond evolves over time. In other words, one's ability to act and ideas for potential action change in and through collaborative engagements with others. Importantly, ability is not synonymous with ableism. People with recognized disabilities have numerous abilities, including many from which those without diagnosed disabilities can learn.

In order to emphasize the ability aspect of response-ability, music educators and students might invite local advocates for the issue at hand, including students and fellow educators, to the event. Advocates could speak during the musical event and set up informational tables, noting organization needs and specific actionable steps. They could provide input on the overall format of the musical event, including possible response opportunities.

In summary, disruptive artistic endeavors that have the potential to challenge problematic capitalist inequities emphasize participants' responses and develop their agency to act. They often involve lingering, interruptive affective flows while foregrounding attention to contemporary material conditions. Rather than succumbing to defeat, such artistic endeavors promote agentive hopefulness that the world can be otherwise. While the aforementioned ideas rely on existing institutions, teachers and students might also ask, What would it mean to disrupt material inequities more broadly?

DISRUPTING MUSIC EDUCATION INSTITUTIONS AND BEYOND

Disrupting material inequities at all levels involves foregrounding the redistribution of resources. While music educators and students challenging capitalist inequities need not agree about exactly how money and other goods should be allocated, they would denounce the notion that societies necessitate clear economic winners and losers—those who succeed financially and those who eke out a living with limited finances. Within P-12 schools, school districts, and state education departments, the first and foremost question would be how much money is being spent on each child's music education. Funds would be redistributed so that the wealthiest schools and districts receive the least, and the poorest receive the most.

Within individual music programs, no money would go to supplying resources like marching band props or show choir costumes, which often serve already well-off students, until all interested students received access to instruments, music technology, private lessons, and other resources often attained only by financially privileged students. Likewise, collegiate merit scholarships would be eliminated; financial need would be the sole criterion for determining the distribution of funds. Rather than wealthy community members determining what resources less financially well-off individuals need, stakeholders receiving redistributed resources would play a key role in deciding their uses.

Collegiate music degree admissions requirements also necessitate reconsideration. Changes to audition repertoire and skill sets alone may have little impact on capitalist inequities. Aiming to admit fifty popular music makers and fifty classical music makers rather than one hundred classical music makers simply changes who is excluded. While such action may initially enable the admittance of lower socioeconomic class students, who engage in popular music making absent formal instruction, it ultimately creates a new sorting mechanism more financially well-off families can learn how to exploit. Students from middle- and upper-class families can invest in resources and experiences that enable them to excel at popular music–making audition processes just as easily as they can classical music ones.

Instead, the potential for one's musical endeavors to disrupt capitalist inequities might serve as a primary criterion for admission to schools of music. Music faculty might consider a portfolio assessment in which students provide evidence of not only their music making but also their community engagement, including its potential to disrupt capitalist inequities within local contexts. While genre of music and types of musical practices would inevitably inform with whom and how community interactions occurred, the impact of disruptions would remain a key admission consideration.

Given the limited agency of the arts to directly challenge capitalism, the music performance major would be replaced with a community music education major focused on response-able disruptions. Rather than mainly attending to inequities within schools of music, response-able music majors would strive to challenge those within society more broadly. Given that "people are (generally) insufficiently aware of matters of common concern and undereducated about 'the public,'" collegiate schools of music might enact Ana Vujanovic's suggestion of requiring students to take political education coursework.[43]

Community music education majors would aim for political outcomes, using music making to support and sustain efforts that educate youth and adults about material inequities.[44] For example, response-able community music education majors admitted because they disrupted inequities in their home neighborhoods might build on those efforts by initiating weekly musical gatherings alongside discussions, led by community leaders, about local issues and potential actions. Degree seekers would also be encouraged to develop their expertise in fields that have the potential to challenge capitalism more impactfully, such as politics, community organizing, and environmental studies. Although some readers may consider these proposed ideas unrealistic, I wonder, when asked if you think substantial changes within and beyond capitalist systems are possible, how do you respond?

In the spirit of *Choose Your Own Adventure* books, turn (or return) to chapter 5 to playfully examine surviving under capitalism. To consider resisting capitalist inequities, move to chapter 6. Alternatively, visit chapter 4 to explore how music education might contribute to more equitable thriving within capitalism. Although continuing onto chapter 8 will not necessarily provide closure, chapter 8 includes an investigation of the potential role of popular music in relation to thriving within, surviving under, resisting, and challenging capitalism.

NOTES

1. Theodor Adorno, *Aesthetic Theory*, trans. Robert Hullot-Kentor (Minneapolis: University of Minnesota Press, 1997), 22.

2. Adorno, *Aesthetic Theory*, 237.

3. See the "A Brief History of Capitalism" section of chapter 1.

4. Adorno, *Aesthetic Theory*, 46.

5. Sianne Ngai, *Ugly Feelings* (Cambridge, MA: Harvard University Press, 2005).

6. Ngai, *Ugly Feelings*, 14.

7. Ngai, *Ugly Feelings*, 10.

8. Ngai, *Ugly Feelings*, 11.

9. Naomi Klein, *The Shock Doctrine: The Rise of Disaster Capitalism* (New York: Metropolitan Books, 2007).

10. Clayton M. Christensen, Michael E. Raynor, and Rory McDonald, "What Is Disruptive Innovation?" *Harvard Business Review* 93, no. 12 (2015): 4.

11. Christensen, Raynor, and McDonald, "What Is Disruptive Innovation?" 5.

12. Lana Barkin, Jenner Furst, and Jed Lipinski, *Fyre Fraud*, directed by Jenner Furst and Julia Willoughby Nason (United States: Hulu, 2019), film. The promotional video can be viewed at https://www.youtube.com/watch?v=mz5kY3RsmKo.

13. Hua Hsu, "That Feeling When: What Affect Theory Teaches about the New Age of Anxiety," *New Yorker*, March 25, 2019, 62–64.

14. I am grateful to Emmett O'Leary for bringing this point to my attention.

15. Joseph Abramo, "Whence Culture and Epistemology? Dialectical Materialism and Music Education," *Philosophy of Music Education Review* 29, no. 2 (2021): 155–73.

16. Donna J. Haraway, *Staying with Trouble: Making Kin in the Chthulucene* (Durham, NC: Duke University Press, 2016), 2.

17. Hollie Harding, "Extracts from Melting, Shifting, Liquid World," October 25, 2019, video, 5:15, https://www.youtube.com/watch?v=em2fisXdpRo&t=115s.

18. Haraway, *Staying with Trouble*, 10. Here Haraway is not just referencing string figures but what she calls "sf." She defines *sf* as "a sign for science fiction, speculative feminism, science fantasy, speculative fabulation, science fact, and also, string figures."

19. Lowkey, "The Death of Neoliberalism," August 19, 2017, video, 3:07, https://www.youtube.com/watch?v=aWafMuQZ-t8. I would like to thank Jeremiah Sanders for introducing me to this video.

20. Little Kids Rock, "Frequently Asked Questions," accessed July 8, 2021, https://www.littlekidsrock.org/about/faq/.

21. Ngai, *Ugly Feelings*, 11.

22. I take the idea of a string figure from Haraway, *Staying with Trouble*.

23. Fyre Festival, "Announcing Fyre Festival," January 12, 2017, video, 1:42, https://www.youtube.com/watch?v=mz5kY3RsmKo.

24. Ngai, *Ugly Feelings*, 346.

25. Ngai, *Ugly Feelings*, 36.

26. David Harvey, *A Companion to Marx's Capital: The Complete Edition* (Brooklyn: Verso Books, 2018), 251.

27. DJ CAVEM, "Sprout That Life," May 12, 2019, video, 3:10, https://www.youtube.com/watch?v=IB2IeaoT-bw.

28. Slavoj Žižek, *Like a Thief in Broad Daylight: Power in the Era of Post-human Capitalism* (New York: Seven Stories Press, 2018), 254. While Žižek attributes this idea to Badiou, he does not provide a citation to Badiou.

29. Haraway, *Staying with Trouble*, 2.

30. Clarissa Hayward, "Disruption: What Is It Good For?" *Journal of Politics* 82, no. 2 (2020): 448.

31. Hayward, "Disruption," 454.

32. Hayward, "Disruption," 449.

33. Hayward, "Disruption," 459.

34. Hayward, "Disruption," 449.

35. Rebecca Rivas, "Demonstrators 'Disrupt' STL Symphony Singing a 'Requiem for Mike Brown,'" October 5, 2014, video, 2:11, https://www.youtube.com/watch?v=T_7ErkQFduQ.

36. Hayward, "Disruption," 454.

37. I adapted this idea from a graduate violin recital I saw Morganne Aaberg give at Indiana University in spring 2021.

38. Hayward, "Disruption," 458.

39. Hayward, "Disruption," 448.

40. Haraway, *Staying with Trouble*, 55.

41. Alain Badiou, *The Century*, trans. Alberto Toscano (Malden, MA: Polity Press, 2007), 21.

42. Karen Barad, *Meeting the Universe Halfway: Quantum Physics and the Entanglement of Matter and Meaning* (Durham, NC: Duke University Press, 2007), 141.

43. Ana Vujanovic, "Art as a Bad Public Good," in *Artistic Citizenship: Artistry, Social Responsibility, and Ethical Praxis*, ed. David J. Elliott, Marissa Silverman, and Wayne D. Bowman (New York: Oxford University Press, 2016), 118.

44. This suggestion was inspired by Olúfẹ́mi Táíwò, *Elite Capture: How the Powerful Took over Identity Politics (and Everything Else)* (Chicago: Haymarket Books, 2022), 110.

EIGHT

RECONSIDERING POPULAR MUSIC MAKING

Choosing Hopeful Adventures

THIS BOOK CENTERS ON EXPLAINING four potential ways music educators and students might position themselves in relation to inequitable capitalist economic practices. Thriving within capitalism may involve fast-moving, ever-expanding affective flows. EXCITEMENT combines deep skills with **UNIQUE** contributions that Rouse, and Captivate! Dominate, BIGGER, BIGGEST, MOOOO RRRRRRR EEEEEEEEEEE

Surviving under capitalism might involve resonant composing and play-full affective flows. Dancing joyously, music makers imagine, dream, and uncover childlike wonder. "Why stop?" they say; we want to continue:😜

Resisting capitalist ills can involve dialogic affective flows that witness material inequities.

"Who is missing from the music?" Amanda Gorman writes.

"So many," I say, listening further.

"To challenge settler colonial perception requires reorienting the form by which we share knowledge" states Dylan Robinson.[1]

Who will join me in this reorientation? What can we create together?

Artistic DIS- ruPT- I o N! Can contribute to the challenging of capitalist inequities, but it necessitates s l o w i n g and intro spection. Which side *are you on?* Take a SIDE! - but the arts alone **accomplish little**, so JOIN PoLITiCAl organizations.

The uncritical following of any one trajectory treats the world as fixed and unspeaking, undermining opportunities for resonant responses reliant on adaptation and transformation. In other words, regardless of the positionality, unexamined single paths reinforce capitalist alienation. While music educators and students may feel drawn to some of these potential positionalities more than others, all have value at different times and places.

As noted throughout this text, the four potentialities metaphorically function as paths in a *Choose Your Own Adventure* book. In such books, characters are defined not by single decisions but by a range of possibilities. Leslie Jamison explains: "Going back is the point—not the making but the *re*making of choices."[2] Likewise, music educators and students might foster resonant relationships with each other and their communities through questioning *when* to select a given positionality. Such choices are always temporary and open to revision.

Moreover, the joy of *Choose Your Own Adventure* books comes not from amassing possible adventures—which would mirror capitalist accumulation practices—but from letting go in order to experience each adventure anew. When rereading a *Choose Your Own Adventure* book, keeping the initially chosen ending in mind undermines the richness of subsequent adventures. Likewise, trying to hold onto prior affective flows when enacting different positionalities minimizes opportunities to experience the depth and potential of each unique journey. In order to experience various sequences of musical and pedagogical events, teachers and students might focus on being fully present and responsive to the adventure at hand.

Unlike *Choose Your Own Adventures* books, these four positionalities center the ethical aims of greater material equity and resonant engagements. Given that these ethical ideals promote similarities across the four positionalities, music educators can transfer and build on previous ethical actions. While the nature of musical engagement may change along varying adventures, music programs might be grounded in and defined by ethical aims.

A key argument in this book is that music genre alone does not determine to what extent practices reinforce or challenge capitalist inequities. A popular song can create profit for capitalist producers, and teachers and students can use it in a disruptive protest that awakens awareness about economic disparities. Classical music making can reinforce the self-aggrandizement key to capitalist branding, and it can serve to jolt participants from otherwise unconsidered routines. As such, I propose that music educators and students interested in understanding their present and potential future relationships with capitalist practices focus on affective flows rather than genre.

This does not mean they should never consider the role of music genre or type of musical practice. For example, imagine a music educator who aims to strengthen students' survival under capitalism by inciting playful affective flows solely through classical music making practices. Since such action likely limits students' opportunities to find resonant composing they deem joyful and meaningful, it undermines more robust surviving.

MAYBE POPULAR MUSIC WILL SAVE US: THE ROLE OF GENRE

Following attention to affective flows and ethical commitments, determinations about music genres and types of musical practices are key secondary concerns. Given the title of this book, I explore how popular music making might interface with each of the aforementioned positionalities. The same logic could reveal how other genres and practices could support each positionality. I again utilize Music Will's definition of popular music as encompassing genres ranging from rock and pop to R&B, Latin, rap, and country music.[3]

Thriving within capitalism ultimately involves reaching larger and larger audiences through one's artistic endeavors. As such, thriving necessitates considering not just what students find relevant but what larger communities deem relevant. Since popular music making practices by definition reach a large group of people, they may serve a key place in thriving-focused classrooms. Yet because thriving within capitalism also demands that students develop unique skills, teachers and students might focus on specific subsets of popular music or combine popular music practices with robust skill attainment in another music genre or practice. In order to combat existing material inequities, teachers might favor the musical needs and interests of lower socioeconomic class students, which may involve particular forms of popular music making.

The playful composing important for surviving under capitalism involves music making students find personally meaningful. Since popular music making resonates with a wide range of people, it may serve as an important starting point for playful composing. Yet since producers aim to capture consumers' attention, students who focus only on the popular music they encounter on the radio or social media may end up favoring music that captivates them rather than facilitates their development of unique expressive capacities. As such, teachers might complement popular music making students experience outside formal music teaching and learning settings with sustained engagements in different musical practices students and communities could also find meaningful.

Resisting capitalist inequities involves dialogic music making that raises students' awareness about material injustices. A few popular music makers, like Kendrick Lamar, have created provocative artistic events that encourage participants to confront inequitable systems, such as the continuing effects of slavery and racial segregation in the United States. Yet popular music making often foregrounds participants' comfort; songs that overtly challenge material inequities rarely become popular. In addition to seeking out popular music making that addresses inequities, teachers could search for less well-known tunes by popular artists that address racism and other capitalism-related ills. Teachers can complement such practices with other genres and with music creation, which could draw on popular music practices.

The slowness and inward focus of disruptive artistic endeavors that contribute to the challenging of capitalist inequities contrast the upbeat nature of much popular music making. Yet creations within some subsets of popular music making, such as rap, hip-hop, and independent songwriting, may exhibit such qualities. Additionally, since challenging capitalist inequities necessitates response-able disruptions, decisions about musical content necessitate considering how audience members might react. In some situations, the pervasive nature of popular songs and stylistic elements may encourage audience attentiveness, making responses more likely. In other contexts, the familiarity of popular music making may incentivize audiences to tune it out, and therefore less popular genres may have greater potential to spark responses.

Popular music making can play a key role in any of these four positionalities. While aspects of Western art music making can also contribute to each positionality, popular music making has equal if not more promise in many parts of the world, particularly for the thriving and surviving positionalities. Moreover, incorporating students' and communities' musical traditions serves an important role in the thriving, surviving, and resisting positionalities. As such, culturally sustaining pedagogies can complement main concepts described in this text.[4] However, culturally sustaining pedagogies alone do not necessarily provide the depth of creative expression needed for surviving or the attention to material inequities needed for dialogic witnessing. They also rarely incite the response-able disruptions important for more directly challenging capitalism-related inequities.

HOPE IS A DECISION

Throughout the process of writing this book, two quotations have stuck in my mind. The first is a statement by Mark Fisher: "It's easier to imagine the end of the world than the end of capitalism."[5] Through this research, I have come to understand the intimate relationship between capitalist systems and contemporary humanity. What started out as a surface-level observation—that economic systems necessarily inform music education endeavors—became a profound realization about how much of life, ranging from key values to a vast range of injustices, derives from or at minimum mirrors capitalist economic practices.

At times, writing this book has depressed me. If capitalism demands endless accumulation, racism, sexism, and other ills, and if I cannot imagine the end of capitalism, then why spend time thinking about it? Driven by the insatiable curiosity to understand cultural life more broadly, I take comfort in the fact that I would rather know about systems that guide and limit humanity than remain unaware.

These newfound understandings partly explain why many contemporary social justice–focused music education endeavors have little impact beyond the classroom. Calling for diversity and inclusion within capitalist systems merely changes who is exploited; the pyramidal structures themselves necessitate reimagining. The more people who understand the economic nature of injustices, the more potential exists for collaborative actions aimed at underlying causes of material inequities. While I cannot necessarily imagine an end to capitalism, I can imagine capitalist systems that, working in tension with collective demands, foster less severe economic disparities.

When I began writing this book, I thought I would ultimately hope for readers to prioritize the chapter on challenging capitalism. Although I care deeply about challenging capitalist inequities, I have found myself most inspired by the surviving chapter. If one cannot imagine the end of capitalism, then they need not feel ashamed for at times prioritizing their own survival, particularly since capitalist systems incentivize P-12 and collegiate institutions to demand ever-increasing quantities of underpaid and unpaid labor. Teachers and students can justify spending more time on playful composing and less time on voluntary thriving-focused work. Although I am not advocating for the unbridled self-interest on which capitalism relies, individuals need not sacrifice their own health and well-being for a system that will never fully reward their efforts.

Moreover, music making has existed in all known human cultures, including ones prior to the formation of capitalist economic practices. Should groups coalesce around capitalist alternatives, then I see no reason why such societies would forgo music making. Music making does not need capitalism to survive. This gives me hope, which brings me to a second quotation.

Throughout the process of authoring this book, I continually returned to a statement by Japanese Buddhist philosopher Daisaku Ikeda: "Hope . . . is a decision."[6] Teachers and students cannot choose the economic system into which they are born, and they ultimately have minimal chance of drastically improving their place within it. Yet they can choose "to believe in the limitless dignity and possibilities of both ourselves and others."[7] Thriving within, surviving under, resisting, and challenging capitalist ills all necessitate hope.[8]

Jamison explains that *Choose Your Own Adventure* books give "a way to understand that no ending is really an ending. After every ending, you have to figure out what to do next."[9] Understanding thriving, surviving, resisting, and challenging as returning possibilities rather than singular ends provides hope that teachers and students can continue adventuring in ways meaningful to their changing contexts and circumstances.

I find the notion that hope is a decision particularly important in relation to Slajov Žižek's assertion that contemporary censorship does not crush actual resistance but rather crushes hope.[10] Instead of giving into habits and complacency, teachers and students can create hope by "digging deeper within, searching for even a small glimmer of light."[11] If one spends their limited time on earth being unhopeful, then capitalism really has won.

When teachers and students feel overwhelmed by the limits that capitalism places on them, they might focus not on immediate obstacles but on radical imaginings.[12] Ikeda clarifies: "Real hope is found in committing ourselves to vast goals and dreams—dreams such as a world without war and violence, a world where everyone can live in dignity."[13] The hopeful illumination of such ends can reveal small steps forward that contribute toward them.

Ikeda notes that young people tend to have a particular vitality and hopefulness.[14] While teachers need not hide the difficult realities of capitalism from students, they might avoid extinguishing students' hope in their ability to address them. Educators might draw inspiration from whatever hopeful energy those not yet worn down by life under capitalism bring to their musical engagements. Artistic endeavors can provide an opportunity to be both within and beyond one's time.[15] By foregrounding resonance and material equity, educators and students can look beyond the present historic moment and toward more hopeful presents and futures.

In the spirit of *Choose Your Own Adventure* books, this ending is not really an ending but rather an opportunity for the next adventure to begin. Will that adventure involve more resonant and equitable thriving, surviving, resisting, or challenging? I hopefully invite you to decide.

NOTES

1. Dylan Robinson, *Hungry Listening: Resonant Theory for Indigenous Sound Studies* (Minneapolis: University of Minnesota Press, 2020), 15.
2. Leslie Jamison, "Now What? The Enduring Hold of Choose Your Own Adventure Books," *New Yorker*, September 19, 2022, 36.

3. Music Will, "About Music Will," *Music Will*, accessed June 23, 2023, https://musicwill.org/about/.

4. Django Paris and H. Samy Alim, eds., *Culturally Sustaining Pedagogies: Teaching and Learning for Justice in a Changing World* (New York: Teachers College Press, 2017).

5. Mark Fisher, *Capitalist Realism: Is There No Alternative?* (London: Zero Books, 2009), 1.

6. Daisaku Ikeda, *Hope Is a Decision: Selected Essays* (Santa Monica, CA: Middleway Press, 2017), 4.

7. Ikeda, *Hope Is a Decision*, 4–5.

8. Alexandra Kertz-Welzel has elaborated on the importance of hope for music education. She explains that "hope in education can certainly be a powerful attitude aiming toward sustainable social transformations." Alexandra Kertz-Welzel, *Rethinking Music Education & Social Change* (New York: Oxford University Press, 2022), 127.

9. Jamison, "Now What?" 45.

10. Slavoj Žižek, *Like a Thief in Broad Daylight: Power in the Era of Post-human Capitalism* (New York: Seven Stories Press, 2018), 254.

11. Ikeda, *Hope Is a Decision*, 6.

12. See, for example, Max Haiven and Alex Khasnabish, *The Radical Imagination* (London: Zed Books, 2014).

13. Ikeda, *Hope Is a Decision*, 7–8.

14. Ikeda, *Hope Is a Decision*, 10.

15. Alain Badiou, *The Century*, trans. Alberto Toscano (Malden, MA: Polity Press, 2007), 21.

SELECTED BIBLIOGRAPHY

Abramo, Joseph. "The Phantasmagoria of Competition in School Ensembles." *Philosophy of Music Education Review* 23, no. 2 (2017): 150–70.

———. "What Does Culture Have to Do with Social Justice?" Presentation. Society for Music Teacher Education Symposium. Virtual. September 25, 2021.

———. "Whence Culture and Epistemology? Dialectical Materialism and Music Education." *Philosophy of Music Education Review* 29, no. 2 (2021): 155–73.

Abramo, Joseph, and Cara Faith Bernard. "Barriers to Access and University Schools of Music: A Collective Case Study of Urban High School Students of Color and Their Teachers." *Bulletin of the Council for Research in Music Education* 226 (2020): 7–26.

Adorno, Theodor. *Aesthetic Theory*. Translated by Robert Hullot-Kentor. Minneapolis: University of Minnesota Press, 1997.

———. *The Culture Industry: Selected Essays on Mass Culture*. Edited by J. M. Bernstein. New York: Routledge, 1991.

Ahmed, Sara. *What's the Use*? Durham, NC: Duke University Press, 2019.

Allsup, Randall. "The Eclipse of Higher Education or Problems Preparing Artists in a Mercantile World." *Music Education Research* 17, no. 3 (2015): 251–61.

———. *Remixing the Classroom*. Bloomington: Indiana University Press, 2016.

Allsup, Randall, and Heidi Westerlund. "Methods and Situational Ethics in Music Education." *Action, Criticism, and Theory for Music Education* 11, no. 1 (2012): 124–48.

Anable, Aubrey. "Labor/Leisure." In *Time: A Vocabulary of the Present*, edited by J. Burges and A. J. Elias, 192–208. New York: New York University Press, 2016.

Anderson, Elizabeth. "Education for Democracy in an Age of Political Polarization." Philosophy of Education Society. March 4, 2023. Video, 79:36. https://drive.google.com/file/d/1B1F1qlmnX3jZi69LSFy5dLB_40oBunAJ/.

———. “What Is the Point of Equality?” *Ethics* 109, no. 2 (January 1999): 287–337.

Angel-Alvarado, Rolando, Bayron Gárate-González, and Isabel Quiroga-Fuentes. “Insurrection in Chile: The Effects of Neoliberalism from a Music Education Perspective.” *Action, Criticism, and Theory for Music Education* 20, no. 3 (2021): 108–31.

Apple, Michael. *Official Knowledge: Democratic Education in a Conservative Age*. New York: Routledge, 2014.

Aróstegui, José Luis. “Implications of Neoliberalism and Knowledge Economy for Music Education.” *Music Education Research* 22, no. 1 (2020): 42–53.

Attali, Jacques. *Noise: The Political Economy of Music*. Translated by Brian Massumi. Minneapolis: University of Minnesota Press, 1985.

Badiou, Alain. *The Century*. Translated by Alberto Toscano. Malden, MA: Polity Press, 2007.

———. *The Communist Hypothesis*. Translated by David Macey and Steve Corcoran. Brooklyn: Verso Books, 2010.

Barad, Karen. *Meeting the Universe Halfway: Quantum Physics and the Entanglement of Matter and Meaning*. Durham, NC: Duke University Press, 2007.

Bates, Vincent. “Music Education, Neoliberal Social Reproduction, and Play.” *Action, Criticism, and Theory for Music Education* 20, no. 3 (2021): 92–93.

———. “Standing at the Intersection of Race and Class in Music Education.” *Action, Criticism, and Theory for Music Education* 18, no. 1 (2019): 117–60.

———. “Sustainable School Music for Poor, White, Rural Students.” *Action, Criticism, and Theory for Music Education* 10, no. 2 (2011): 100–27. http://act.maydaygroup.org/articles/Bates10_2.pdf.

Benedict, Cathy. “Capitalist Rationality: Comparing the Lure of the Infinite.” *Philosophy of Music Education Review* 21, no. 1 (2013): 8–22.

———. *Music and Social Justice: A Guide for Elementary Educators*. New York: Oxford University Press, 2021.

———. “Processes of Alienation: Marx, Orff and Kodaly.” *British Journal of Music Education* 26, no. 2 (2009): 213–24.

Benedict, Cathy, and Jared O’Leary. “Reconceptualizing ‘Music Making’: Music Technology and Freedom in the Age of Neoliberalism.” *Action, Criticism, and Theory for Music Education* 18, no. 1 (2019): 26–43.

Blank, Steve, and Bob Dorf. *The Startup Owner’s Manual: The Step-by-Step Guide for Building a Great Company*. Pescadero, CA: K & S Ranch, 2012.

Bourdieu, Pierre. *Distinction: A Social Critique of the Judgement of Taste*. Translated by Richard Nice. Cambridge, MA: Harvard University Press, 1984.

Bowman, Wayne. “Music as Ethical Encounter (Charles Leonhard Lecture, University of Illinois).” *Bulletin of the Council for Research in Music Education* 151 (2001): 11–20.

Britton, Allen, Arnold Broido, and Charles Gary. "The Tanglewood Declaration," in *Documentary Report of the Tanglewood Symposium*. Edited by Robert A. Choate. Washington, DC: Music Educators National Conference, 1968.

Brown, Stuart. *Play: How It Shapes the Brain, Opens the Imagination, and Invigorates the Soul*. New York: Penguin Group, 2009.

Brown, Wendy. *In the Ruins of Neoliberalism: The Rise of Antidemocratic Politics in the West*. New York: Columbia University Press, 2018.

Bull, Anna. *Class, Control, and Classical Music*. New York: Oxford University Press, 2019.

Campbell, Patricia Shehan, David Myers, and Ed Sarath. "Transforming Music Study from Its Foundations: A Manifesto for Progressive Change in the Undergraduate Preparation of Music Majors." *College Music Society*. 2016. https://www.music.org/pdf/pubs/tfumm/TFUMM.pdf.

Catmull, Ed. *Creativity, Inc.: Overcoming the Unseen Forces That Stand in the Way of True Inspiration*. Edited by Amy Wallace. New York: Random House, 2014.

Cheng, William. *Loving Music Till It Hurts*. New York: Oxford University Press, 2019.

Christensen, Clayton M., Michael E. Raynor, and Rory McDonald. "What Is Disruptive Innovation?" *Harvard Business Review* 93, no. 12 (2015): 4–53.

Churchill, Warren N., and Cara Faith Bernard. "Disability and the Ideology of Ability: How Might Music Educators Respond?" *Philosophy of Music Education Review* 28, no. 1 (2020): 24–46.

Cole, David N. "Leave No Trace: How It Came to Be." *International Journal of Wilderness* 24, no. 3 (2018): 54–65.

Colwell, Richard. "A Peek at an International Perspective on Assessment." In *Music Education Entering the 21st Century*, edited by Patricia Martin Shand, 17–32. Western Australia: International Society for Music Education, 2004.

Damasio, Antonio R. *The Feeling of What Happens: Body and Emotion in the Making of Consciousness*. Orlando: Harcourt, 1999.

Elliott, David J. *Music Matters: A New Philosophy of Music Education*. New York: Oxford University Press, 1995.

Elliott, David J., and Marissa Silverman. *Music Matters: A Philosophy of Music Education*. 2nd ed. New York: Oxford University Press, 2015.

Dewey, John. *The Public and Its Problems*. Athens, OH: Swallow Press, 1927.

Dunn, Damaris, and Bettina L. Love. "Antiracist Language Arts Pedagogy Is Incomplete without Black Joy." *Racial Literacy: Implications for Curriculum, Pedagogy, and Policy* 1 (2021): 69–70.

Dweck, Carol. *Self-Theories*. Lillington, NC: Taylor & Francis, 2000.

Ellsworth, Elizabeth. "Why Doesn't This Feel Empowering? Working through the Repressive Myths of Critical Pedagogy." *Harvard Educational Review* 59, no. 3 (1989): 297–324.

Elpus, Kenneth, and Carlos R. Abril. "Who Enrolls in High School Music? A National Profile of U.S. Students, 2009–2013." *Journal of Research in Music Education* 67, no. 3 (2019): 323–38.

Fautley, Martin. "Assessment Policy and Practice in Secondary Schools in the English National Curriculum." In *The Oxford Handbook of Assessment Policy and Practice in Music Education, Volume 1*, 219–32. New York: Oxford University Press, 2019.

Federici, Silvia. *Beyond the Periphery of the Skin: Rethinking, Remaking, and Reclaiming the Body in Contemporary Capitalism*. Brooklyn: PM Press, 2020.

———. *Patriarchy of the Wage: Notes on Marx, Gender, and Feminism*. Brooklyn: PM Press, 2021.

Fink, Eugen. *Play as Symbol of the World*. Translated by Ian Alexander Moore and Christopher Turner. Bloomington: Indiana University Press, 2016.

Fisher, Mark. *Capitalist Realism: Is There No Alternative?* London: Zero Books, 2009.

Fitzpatrick, Kate R. "Cultural Diversity and the Formation of Identity: Our Role as Music Teachers." *Music Educators Journal* 98, no. 4 (2012): 53–59.

Foucault, Michel. *The Birth of Biopolitics*. Edited by Michel Senellart. Translated by Graham Burchell. New York: Palgrave Macmillan, 2008.

———. *Discipline and Punish: The Birth of the Prison*. Translated by Alan Sheridan. New York: Vintage Books, 1995.

———. *Power/Knowledge: Selected Interviews and Other Writings, 1972–1997*. Edited by Colin Gordon. Translated by Colin Gordon, Leo Marshall, John Mepham, and Kate Soper. New York: Pantheon Books, 1980.

Fraser, Nancy. *Cannibal Capitalism: How Our System Is Devouring Democracy, Care, and the Planet—and What We Can Do about It*. Brooklyn: Verso Books, 2022.

———. *The Old Is Dying and the New Cannot Be Reborn*. Brooklyn: Verso Books, 2019.

Freire, Paulo, and Donaldo P. Macedo. "A Dialogue: Culture, Language, and Race." *Harvard Educational Review* 65, no. 3 (1995): 377–402.

Gago, Verónica. "Financialization of Popular Life and the Extractive Operations of Capital: A Perspective from Argentina." *South Atlantic Quarterly* 114, no. 1 (2015): 11–28.

Goble, J. Scott. "Neoliberalism and Music Education: An Introduction." *Action, Criticism, and Theory for Music Education* 20, no. 3 (2021): 1–18. https://doi.org/10.22176/act20.3.1.

Goehr, Lydia. *The Imaginary Museum of Musical Works: An Essay in the Philosophy of Music*. New York: Oxford University Press, 2007.

Gould, Elizabeth. "Social Justice in Music Education: The Problematic of Democracy." *Music Education Research* 9, no. 2 (2007): 229–40.

———. "Women Working in Music Education: The War Machine." *Philosophy of Music Education Review* 17, no. 2 (2009): 126–43.

Greene, Maxine. "Imagining Futures: The Public School and Possibility." *Journal of Curriculum Studies* 32, no. 2 (2000): 267–80.
———. *Variations on a Blue Guitar: The Lincoln Center Institute Lectures on Aesthetic Education*. New York: Teachers College Press, 2001.
Haiven, Max, and Alex Khasnabish. *The Radical Imagination*. London: Zed Books, 2014.
Hansen, David T., and Rebecca Sullivan. "What Renders a Witness Trustworthy? Ethical and Curricular Notes on a Mode of Educational Inquiry." *Studies in Philosophy and Education* 41 (2022): 151–72.
Haraway, Donna J. *Staying with Trouble: Making Kin in the Chthulucene*. Durham, NC: Duke University Press, 2016.
Harvey, David. *A Companion to Marx's Capital: The Complete Edition*. Brooklyn: Verso Books, 2018.
———. *Seventeen Contradictions and the End of Capitalism*. New York: Oxford University Press, 2014.
Hayek, Friedrich A. *The Road to Serfdom*. New York: Routledge, 1941.
Hayward, Clarissa. "Disruption: What Is It Good For?" *Journal of Politics* 82, no. 2 (2020): 448–59.
Heath, Chip, and Dan Heath. *Made to Stick: Why Some Ideas Survive and Others Die*. New York: Random House, 2007.
Heimonen, Marja. "'Bildung' and Music Education: A Finnish Perspective." *Philosophy of Music Education Review* 22, no. 2 (2014): 188–208.
Hertz, Noreena. *The Lonely Century: How to Restore Human Connection in a World That's Pulling Apart*. New York: Currency, 2021.
Hess, Juliet. "'Putting a Face on It': The Trouble with Storytelling for Social Justice in Music Education." *Philosophy of Music Education Review* 29, no. 1 (2021): 67–87.
Hochschild, Arlie. *Strangers in Their Own Land: Anger and Morning on the American Right*. New York: New Press, 2016.
hooks, bell. *Where We Stand: Class Matters*. New York: Routledge, 2000.
Hsu, Hua. "That Feeling When: What Affect Theory Teaches about the New Age of Anxiety." *New Yorker*, March 25, 2019.
Hudis, Peter. "Marx's Concept of Socialism." In *The Oxford Handbook of Karl Marx*, edited by Matt Vidal, Tony Smith, Tomás Rotta, and Paul Prew, 757–72. New York: Oxford University Press, 2018.
Hyde, Lewis. *The Gift: Creativity and the Artist in the Modern World*. New York: Vintage Books, 2007.
Ikeda, Daisaku. *Hope Is a Decision: Selected Essays*. Santa Monica, CA: Middleway Press, 2017.
Isaacson, Walter. *Steve Jobs*. New York: Simon & Schuster, 2011.

Jamison, Leslie. "Now What? The Enduring Hold of Choose Your Own Adventure Books." *New Yorker*, September 19, 2022.
Jank, Warner. "Didaktik, Bildung, Content: On the Writings of Frede V. Nielsen." *Philosophy of Music Education Review* 22, no. 2 (2014): 113–31.
Kertz-Welzel, Alexandra. *Rethinking Music Education & Social Change*. New York: Oxford University Press. 2022.
Kim, W. Chan, and Renée Mauborgne. *Blue Ocean Strategy Reader*. Boston: Harvard Business Review Press, 2014.
Kimmerer, Robin Wall. *Braiding Sweetgrass: Indigenous Wisdom, Scientific Knowledge and the Teachings of Plants*. Minneapolis, MN: Milkweed Editions, 2013.
Klein, Naomi. *The Shock Doctrine: The Rise of Disaster Capitalism*. New York: Metropolitan Books, 2007.
Krugman, Paul. *Arguing with Zombies*. New York: W. W. Norton, 2021.
Leonardo, Zeus. *Race Frameworks: A Multidimensional Theory of Racism and Education*. New York: Columbia University Press, 2013.
Lipari, Lisbeth. *Listening, Thinking, Being: Toward an Ethics of Attunement*. University Park: Pennsylvania State University Press, 2014.
Louth, J. Paul. "Emphasis and Suggestion versus Musical Taxidermy: Neoliberal Contradictions, Music Education, and the Knowledge Economy." *Philosophy of Music Education Review* 28, no. 2 (2020): 88–107.
———. "Music Education and the Shrinking Public Space." Virtual presentation at International Symposium on the Sociology of Music Education, June 21, 2021.
MacIntyre, Alasdair. *Ethics in the Conflicts of Modernity: An Essay on Desire, Practical Reasoning, and Narrative*. Cambridge: Cambridge University Press, 2016.
Mantie, Roger. *Music, Leisure, Education: Historical and Philosophical Perspectives*. New York: Oxford University Press, 2022.
Marantz, Andrew. "The Left Turn." *New Yorker*, May 31, 2021.
Mark, Michael L., and Charles L. Gary. *A History of American Music Education*. 3rd ed. Lanham, MD: Rowman & Littlefield Education, 2007.
Marx, Karl. *Capital Vol. 1: A Critique of Political Economy*, translated by Ben Fowkes. New York: Penguin, 2004.
———. *Capital Vol. 2*, translated by David Fernach. New York: Penguin, 1993.
———. *Economic and Philosophic Manuscripts of 1844*. Translated by Martin Milligan. Amherst, NY: Prometheus, 1988.
———. "Estranged Labor." *Economic and Philosophical Manuscripts 1844*. Accessed June 27, 2023. https://www.marxists.org/archive/marx/works/1844/manuscripts/labour.htm.
Massumi, Brian. "The Autonomy of Affect." *Cultural Critique* 31 (1995): 83–109.
McCall, Joyce. "'A Peculiar Sensation': Mirroring Du Bois' Path into Predominantly White Institutions in the 21st Century." *Action, Criticism, and Theory for Music Education* 20, no. 4 (2021): 10–44. https://doi.org/10.22176/act20.4.10.

McPhail, Graham, and Jeff McNeill. "Music Education and the Neoliberal Turn in Aotearoa New Zealand." *Action, Criticism, and Theory for Music Education* 20, no. 3 (2021): 44–81.
McRobbie, Angela. *Feminism and the Politics of Resilience: Essays on Gender, Media and the End of Welfare*. Cambridge: Polity, 2020.
Monarrez, Tomás, Brian Kisida, and Matthew Chingos. "Charter School Effects on School Segregation." *Urban Institute*. July 24, 2019. https://www.urban.org/research/publication/charter-school-effects-school-segregation/.
Moore, Marcus J. *The Butterfly Effect: How Kendrick Lamar Ignited the Soul of Black America*. Miami: Atria Books, 2020.
Mouffe, Chantel. *For a Left Populism*. Brooklyn: Verso Books, 2018.
Mullen, Jess. "Music Education for Some: Music Standards at the Nexus of Neoliberal Reforms and Neoconservative Values." *Action Criticism, and Theory for Music Education* 18, no. 1 (2019): 44–67.
Ngai, Sianne. *Our Aesthetic Categories*. Cambridge, MA: Harvard University Press, 2012.
———. *Ugly Feelings*. Cambridge, MA: Harvard University Press, 2005.
Osnos, Evan. "How to Hire a Pop Star for Your Private Party." *New Yorker*, May 29, 2023. https://www.newyorker.com/magazine/2023/06/05/how-to-hire-a-pop-star-for-your-private-party.
Paris, Django, and H. Samy Alim, eds. *Culturally Sustaining Pedagogies: Teaching and Learning for Justice in a Changing World*. New York: Teachers College Press, 2017.
Patel, Raj, and Jason W. Moore. *A History of the World in Seven Cheap Things: A Guide to Capitalism, Nature, and the Future of the Planet*. Oakland: University of California Press, 2018.
Peterson, Richard, and Roger Kerns. "Changing Highbrow Taste: From Snob to Omnivore." *American Sociological Review* 61, no. 5 (1996): 900–907.
Picower, Bree. "Using Their Words: Six Elements of Social Justice Curriculum Design for the Elementary Classroom." *International Journal of Multicultural Education* 14, no. 1 (2012): 1–17.
Powell, Sean Robert. "Competition, Ideology, and the One-Dimensional Music Program." *Action, Criticism, and Theory for Music Education* 20, no. 3 (2021): 19–43.
———. *The Ideology of Competition in School Music*. New York: Oxford University Press, 2023.
Putnam, Robert D. *Bowling Alone: The Collapse and Revival of the American Community*. New York: Simon Schuster, 2000.
Rand, Ayn. *Atlas Shrugged*. New York: Signet, 1996.
———. *The Fountainhead*. New York: Signet, 1971.
Regelski, Thomas. "On 'Methodolatry' and Music Teaching as Critical and Reflective Praxis." *Philosophy of Music Education Review* 10, no. 2 (2002): 102–23.
Reimer, Bennett. *A Philosophy of Music Education*. Hoboken, NJ: Prentice Hall, 1970.

Richerme, Lauren Kapalka. *Complicating, Considering, and Connecting Music Education*. Bloomington: Indiana University Press, 2020.

Rickels, David A. "Nonperformance Variables as Predictors of Marching Band Contest Results." *Bulletin of the Council for Research in Music Education* 194 (2012): 53–72.

Ries, Eric. *The Lean Startup: How Today's Startups Use Continuous Innovation to Create Radically Successful Businesses*. New York: Crown Business, 2011.

Ritchey, Marianna. *Composing Capital: Classical Music in the Neoliberal Era*. Chicago: University of Chicago Press, 2019.

Robinson, Dylan. *Hungry Listening: Resonant Theory for Indigenous Sound Studies*. Minneapolis: University of Minnesota Press, 2020.

Robinson, William. *The Rise of the Global Police State*. London: Pluto Press, 2020.

Rosa, Hartmut. *Resonance: A Sociology of Our Relationship to the World*. Translated by James C. Wagner. Cambridge: Polity Press, 2019.

Sandberg, Sheryl. *Lean In: Women, Work, and the Will to Lead*. Edited by Nell Scovell. New York: Alfred A. Knopf, 2013.

Sandel, Michael. *The Tyranny of Merit: What's Become of the Common Good?* New York: Farrer, Straus and Giroux, 2020.

Schmidt, Patrick. "Ethics or Choosing Complexity in Music Relations." *Action, Criticism, and Theory for Music Education* 11, no. 1 (2012): 149–68.

Seigworth, Gregory J., and Melissa Gregg. "An Inventory of Shimmers." In *The Affect Theory Reader*, edited by Melissa Gregg and Gregory J. Seigworth, 1–25. Durham, NC: Duke University Press, 2010.

Sensoy, Özlem, and Robin, DiAngelo. *Is Everyone Really Equal? An Introduction to Key Concepts in Social Justice Education*. New York: Teachers College Press, 2017.

Silverman, Marissa. "Listening-for Social Justice." In *Giving Voice to Democracy in Music Education*, edited by Lisa C. DeLorenzo, 157–75. New York: Routledge, 2015.

Smith, Gareth Dylan. "Neoliberalism and Symbolic Violence in Higher Music Education." In *Giving Voice to Democracy in Music Education*, edited by Lisa C. DeLorenzo, 65–84. New York: Routledge, 2015.

Stauffer, Sandra, and Margaret Barrett. "Narrative Inquiry in Music Education: Toward Resonant Work." In *Narrative Inquiry in Music Education: Troubling Certainty*, edited by Margaret Barrett and Sandra Stauffer, 19–29. New York: Springer Science+Business Media, 2009.

Stauffer, Sandra, Jill Sullivan, Margaret Schmidt, and Evan Tobias. "Aligning Conceptions and Capacity: Turning Visions into Reality." Presentation. *Society for Music Teacher Education*, Greensboro, North Carolina. September 2013.

Stewart, Lindsey. *The Politics of Black Joy: Zora Neale Hurston and Neo-abolitionism*. Evanston, IL: Northwestern University Press, 2021.

Táíwò, Olúfẹ́mi. *Elite Capture: How the Powerful Took over Identity Politics (and Everything Else)*. Chicago: Haymarket Books, 2022.

Taylor, Timothy. *Music and Capitalism: A History of the Present*. Chicago: University of Chicago Press, 2016.
Thiel, Peter. *Zero to One: Notes on Startups, or How to Build the Future*. Edited by Blake Masters. New York: Crown Business, 2014.
Titmuss, Richard M. *The Gift Relationship: From Human Blood to Social Policy*. New York: New Press, 1997.
Tolentino, Jia. "How TikTok Holds Our Attention." *New Yorker*, September 30, 2019. https://www.newyorker.com/magazine/2019/09/30/how-tiktok-holds-our-attention.
Turino, Thomas. *Music as Social Life: The Politics of Participation*. Chicago: University of Chicago Press, 2008.
Turkle, Sherry. *Reclaiming Conversation: The Power of Talk in a Digital Age*. New York: Penguin Books, 2015.
Vujanovic, Ana. "Art as a Bad Public Good." In *Artistic Citizenship: Artistry, Social Responsibility, and Ethical Praxis*, edited by David J. Elliott, Marissa Silverman, and Wayne D. Bowman, 104–22. New York: Oxford University Press, 2016.
Wheeler-Bell, Quentin. "An Immanent Critique of Critical Pedagogy." *Educational Theory* 69, no. 3 (2019): 265–81.
Woodford, Paul. *Music Education in an Age of Virtuality and Post-truth*. New York: Routledge, 2018.
Žižek, Slavoj. *Like a Thief in Broad Daylight: Power in the Era of Post-human Capitalism*. New York: Seven Stories Press, 2018.

INDEX

Page locators with italics indicate figures and tables

Lauren Kapalka Richerme is Associate Professor of Music Education at the Indiana University Jacobs School of Music. She is author of *Complicating, Considering, and Connecting Music Education* (IUP 2020) and (with Peter Miksza, Julia T. Shaw, Phillip M. Hash, and Donald A. Hodges) of *Music Education Research: An Introduction.*

For Indiana University Press

Tony Brewer, Artist and Book Designer
Allison Chaplin, Acquisitions Editor
Dan Crissman, Editorial Director and Acquisitions Editor
Gary Dunham, Acquisitions Editor and Director
Anna Garnai, Production Coordinator
Sophia Hebert, Assistant Acquisitions Editor
Samantha Heffner, Marketing and Publicity Manager
Katie Huggins, Production Manager
Dave Hulsey, Associate Director and Director of Sales and Marketing
Nancy Lightfoot, Project Manager/Editor
Dan Pyle, Online Publishing Manager
Michael Regoli, Director of Publishing Operations
Stephen Williams, Assistant Director of Marketing
Jennifer Witzke, Senior Artist and Book Designer

www.ingramcontent.com/pod-product-compliance
Lightning Source LLC
Chambersburg PA
CBHW030502070525
26216CB00001B/5
* 9 7 8 0 2 5 3 0 7 2 4 3 6 *